Streakin'

"THE REAL HIGH SCHOOL ADVENTURES
OF A NOT-SO-PLAIN JANE"

BY
Jane Simkins

Cover Design by Annia

Print ISBN: 978-1-54397-319-8

eBook ISBN: 978-1-54397-320-4

For every 8th grader
about to enter high school.

Relax. Parallel parking will be way
more difficult than making friends.

Acknowledgments

Although my name is in the title, *Jane's Journal* would not exist without the confident and creative support, not to mention spell-checking, of these wonderful people:

> Thank you to the Galesburg Register Mail (with a special shout out to Tom Loewy, Tom Martin, and Jane Carlson), who took a chance on a timid teenager and gave her the guts and confidence to share her voice.

> Thank you to my parents who graciously ran grammar and spelling patrol into the wee hours of many Thursday nights. And for doing all the heavy lifting in digging up and compiling these articles and photos into a single document on an old computer using Windows '99. Please know that I'm giving you a standing ovation as I write this.

> Thank you to my grandparents who saved every piece of news with my name in it, but hopefully not that one "article" way in the back of the paper where I received my first speeding ticket. Although, they were so supportive that they'd probably even cheer me on for that one, too.

> Honorary mentions go to my faithful four-legged friend Boomerang and my annoyingly perfect brother John, without whom there'd be no bar for me to reach.

> And of course, to School District #205, home of the Silver Streaks and some of the most dedicated and creative

teachers, coaches and staff anywhere. Your daily diligence to provide guidance and lessons about life in the classrooms, hallways, gyms, and fields on and around West Fremont Street helped a shy freshman grow into an engaging adult. I will be forever in your debt.

Prelude To A Streak

I t was the summer before my freshman year of high school and I was kicking rocks beside the baseball field, waiting for my brother to mosey out of the dug out while Queen's "Another One Bites the Dust" reverberated from atop the concession stand. Waiting for John, or "the golden child," as I referred to him in my head, was a common scenario in the Simkins' household, especially during his senior year.

John was (and still is) a rockstar. Art, sports, music, calculus, breathing, you name it, he's crushing it. One of the most absurd things I've witnessed was watching my brother strum along to his first place "Battle of the Bands" song while wearing his freshly anointed Swirl King crown in the high school gym, where he'd inevitably sink a half-court shot during the half-time show of a girls' varsity basketball game later that year. He was (and still is) a really swell brother, too.

But back to me.

So as I'm standing there in the dust of my brother, the baseball field and Freddie Mercury that summer day, you can imagine my surprise when, through the haze of hot dog steam and Double Bubbles, Tom Loewy, columnist for the Galesburg Register Mail, appeared and approached my mom and me about his idea for a new column about *me*.

Well, not about *me*, entirely. The concept was to follow the journey of a high school student from freshman orientation to senior graduation, through a weekly journal full of her personal fears, failures, triumphs and insecurities, for her classmates, teachers, coaches, crushes and people she'd never even met, to see.

Needless to say, I was totally game.

Throughout my four years of high school, I never missed a "Jane's Journal" deadline. Neither late nights, soggy soccer games, anxiety-riddled Algebra tests, nor the quintessential high school friendship quarrel, stopped me from ending Thursday nights at the family computer with something to say.

Ten years and 161 journal entries later, "Jane's Journal" has become this book. In your hands you hold four years of my personal experiences and processing of those experiences. Be kind. Handle them with care and please forgive Freshman Jane's writing style - she hadn't quite found her voice yet. Spoiler alert: it shows up somewhere after getting her driver's license.

My hope is that you'll read this book, even if it's just once in a while when you need a refreshing flashback to your own high school self. My wish is that you'll share this book with someone Streakin' through high school right now. It's comforting to know your peers are on the same rollercoaster of emotions but sometimes everyone feels safer playing it cool. I think high school Jane would be okay exposing her "uncool" self to them. In fact, I invite everyone to laugh at her expense and to roll their eyes when she tries to sound *super wise* - I do it all the time.

Let's go Streakin'!

Contents

SOPHOMORE YEAR

JUNIOR YEAR

SENIOR YEAR

FRESHMAN YEAR

Getting Ready for High School

AUGUST 27

- -

WOW, these past school years have gone by fast! It seems like just yesterday I was heading off to all-day kindergarten at Silas (Willard) Elementary School, kicking and screaming as my parents struggled to get me out of the van. Now, nine years later, here I am heading off to the Big G - Galesburg High School - and I must admit I'm nervous.

It was pretty tough to decide what classes to take considering there are so many choices, but I finally figured out my freshman course schedule. This year I will be taking biology, English 151, American history, Algebra 1A and 1B, beginning art, band and keyboarding. Geez, that's a lot of classes; hopefully, I won't get lost my first day. Yet, knowing me, I probably will end up having to ask a teacher or upperclassman where my classes are. When I talk to my friends about high school, they say they are feeling about the same way I am - nervous and excited - which kind of makes me feel better.

I guess I never actually realized how busy I'm going to be this school year with band, school, hopefully volleyball, soccer, clubs, and other activities. Gosh, I get overwhelmed just thinking about it. Then again, I guess it's a good thing I'll be busy. Hopefully, being so involved will help me meet new people and make new friends.

First Day of High School

SEPTEMBER 10

My first official day as a high school student began with me waking up late. Immediately, I began rushing around my closet to find the perfect outfit to make that great first impression. After a frantic half-hour of getting ready for school, I sprinted over to my friend Emily's house to catch a ride with her brother.

Practically shakin' in my boots, I walked up the steps to the "Kingdom," or as most call it, Galesburg High School, with a pink notebook, snazzy folder, and Bic No. 2 pencil in hand. I slowly opened the heavy door to the band hall - all seemed pretty normal. That's right, no seven-foot-tall seniors waiting to take my lunch money, no scary teachers with fangs, and no one waiting to drag me in the bathroom with a one-way ticket to "Swirlyville."

I began to think, "maybe I'll be OK and won't get lost or thrown in a dumpster." Confidence continued to build as I marched my way through the halls without much trouble at all. Strangely, school was fun and going to each new class was like opening a cardboard box, contents unknown. Even when I passed my friends in the halls, they looked like they were enjoying themselves, too. Throughout the day, I met some really nice people and for once in a very long time, I actually ate a school lunch. You know what? It was good!

As I waited for my ride on the front steps of GHS, I started to look at the high school as my new home away from home. I felt like an official Silver Streak!

The Story Is There Is No Story

SEPTEMBER 17

- -

NO STORY ON THIS DATE, JANE GIVEN THE WEEK OFF. THIS IS THE only Saturday during the school year in the 4 years that Jane's Journal did not appear in the Galesburg Register-Mail.

Homecoming Dance Here

SEPTEMBER 24

- -

WOW, MY FIRST HIGH SCHOOL DANCE IS ONLY A FEW DAYS AWAY. Buying tickets, getting a dress and organizing dinner plans are only a few of the many preparations for homecoming. The theme is "Cruisin' the Caribbean." There was a fun little dress code for each day of the week, which included: Crazy Hair Day, Pajama Day and Backwards Day.

The popular Powder Puff game was played Wednesday night. The junior and senior girls charged on the field with black paint smeared under their eyes and ponytails tied tight in their hair. The boys, dressed as cheerleaders, assembled on the sideline and tried to figure out how to build a pyramid. The guys even tried to bust a few hilarious gymnastic moves.

It's Thursday as I write this journal entry and I can't wait for the dance. Though I was lucky enough to be asked by a friend, some of my other compadres are going in groups together. I've also heard of some people going by themselves just because they like to strut their stuff or want to see what an actual formal dance is like. I'm guessing that, come Saturday night, a bunch of friends and co-eds will just be shakin' a leg and having a good time, which sounds like fun to me.

I have also been told Galesburg High School has some talented break dancers - which would be pretty entertaining since I can't "bust a move" to save my life. Don't get me wrong, I mean I've learned a few sweet moves from my brother John. He's taught me Fisherman, Grocery

Cart, and Drivin' the Car. But those are pretty much for dancing at home, where no one can see you.

I can't wait to see the plain old gym turned into a tropical getaway. Whether my first dance is a Debbie Downer or a great time, at least I'll be able to say I, Jane Simkins, grooved to the tunes at a Galesburg High School dance.

Homecoming a Journey Away

OCTOBER 1

- -

AS MY FRIEND JAKE AND I WALKED THROUGH THE DOORS OF Galesburg High School to attend Saturday night's homecoming dance, it became immediately apparent we weren't in Galesburg anymore.

When I looked around, I saw huge paper palm trees, paper mache coconuts, colorful tropical flowers and loads of glitter. To the right, in the cafeteria, there were groups of friends and couples having their pictures snapped in front of a sunset background with flowers and more palm trees. In front of me, music was blaring from the gym, which looked really dark from the outside.

Yet, once I stepped through the mysteriously black doorway, I felt as if I really were in the Caribbean. Blue and white streamers were laced back and forth across the ceiling and an amazingly gargantuan pirate ship - with SpongeBob at the top - jutted out from the back wall. As I continued to look upward, I noticed a huge paper mache whale hanging from the ceiling. Refreshments and chairs were located at the balcony so when you were tired from groovin' to the tunes you could take a break and watch the dance from a different view.

When I asked others how their night was going, most agreed that they were having a better time than they had anticipated. As the night went on, I ran into my friends Lindsey, Jenna, and Whitty and they said it was fun to go out to eat with their dates at a nice restaurant.

Most of the night, I danced and had fun with my friends. One even asked a guy she had never met to dance. Later, there were some talented break dancers who executed all kinds of moves that made my back hurt just watching them.

As the night came to a close, no one wanted it to end because of all the fun they were having. While the final song of the night was playing in the background, you could see the sparkle in everyone's eye. Or was it just a stray piece of decorating glitter?

Band Competition Nets a Close Shave

OCTOBER 8

- -

"BAND, TEN HUT!"

Those now-familiar words signaled the beginning of the parade competition last Saturday morning in Washington. The Galesburg Marching Streaks took part in the competition. As we marched up and down the hills along the route, everyone around me looked like wind-up toy soldiers moving to the beat. The atmosphere was amazing; you could feel the excitement from my fellow band members as well as onlookers lined up along the street.

Even students from other high school bands cheered us on. When the parade portion of the competition finished and everyone started to take off their helmets, we changed from a dignified group of musicians back to a sweaty, smelly group of teenagers.

In between parade and field show competitions, we had a chance to watch bands from other schools perform. It was so cool to see how creative bands of all sizes can be with marching and music. We were really pumped up to perform the field show, since Mr. Bredhemier, our director, promised to shave his head if we were awarded Grand Champions.

What a unique way to bring 190 musicians together to achieve a common goal. Once we completed our warm-up in the local school gymnasium, our director delivered his final pep talk. We were all riled up and focused to give a great performance.

We formed up and began marching our way to the field where the bleachers were packed with fans. We started to play our opener and a sudden rush of energy filled me and my mellophone as we began our first selection, "Robin Hood." The hum of drum major Eric Thornson's bagpipe began our second song, "Braveheart." Our third selection, "Barbarian Horde," came through with a "pow" and ripped the temporary silence on the field at the 50-yard line. Our finale started off with a bang when Keegan Siebken busted out his acoustic guitar. "Waw waw waw," sang his guitar to the introduction to "Gladiator."

We marched off the field and assembled in a grassy area behind the bleachers. Mr. B shared with us that he dreamed he woke up the day after the competition bald. As we waited for the results, the tension was so thick around the stadium you could cut it with a knife.

Our band received awards for best drum majors and best drum-line in parade, among others. But the big question remained, who was this year's Grand Champion Band? After a dramatic pause, the judge announced, "And finally ... your 2005 Grand champion is ... GALESBURG!"

Sweaty, smelly and joyous band members immediately started to scream and hug each other. It took so long to get everyone back on the buses and calmed down that our diehard chaperones had to round everyone up. Winning Grand Champion was a defining moment in my freshman marching band career. Seeing my reflection in the bell of my mello and the top of Mr. B's head is priceless.

Glittery Handbags Latest Fashion Fad

OCTOBER 15

- -

AS WE HEAD INTO THE FINAL THREE WEEKS OF THE FIRST QUARTER AT Galesburg High School, I've started to notice some changes in my surroundings. The color of the leaves is becoming more vivid and the daylight hours are getting shorter, but more importantly, there is a new fashion trend hitting the halls of GHS.

Fads or trends spring up in many unusual ways. Remember the hairstyle fad in the 1980s called the "mullet?" Another fashion statement was bellbottoms - jeans worn by our parents in the 70s that live on in some of our own wardrobes today. I will never understand these saggy-baggy pants - let's hope this fad is soon on its way out along with bushy sideburns.

This year's fad, however, is more of an accessory. It's a purse or handbag with tons of shiny, glittery discs attached all over it. These eye-catching knits seem to be hanging from the shoulder of every girl at Galesburg High School.

People have many different opinions about this new rave, both pro and con. Some girls say when they strap on these purses, they can transform any dull outfit into an exciting, flashy one. Good point. Others, however, say that since almost everyone has a sequined satchel, they are no longer unique. I like to think that style is not about what you wear, but how you wear it. Overall, I believe the best advice I've heard is to look beyond the shiny handbags and unique styles to gain a clear view of a person.

As far as fads go, the glitter happy purses will hold a special place in our high school memories, just like the good ole "Macarena," pet rocks, platform shoes and leg warmers. By the way, what exactly is a sea monkey?

Haunted High School More Fun Than Fright

OCTOBER 22

- -

THE CHILL OF FALL IS IN THE AIR, WHICH MEANS OUR GALESBURG High School Student Council is busy working on plans for the annual "Haunted High School," which will take place at GHS from 5 to 7 p.m. on Sunday, Oct. 30.

Planning for such an event begins at our regular 7:00 meeting on Tuesday mornings. Student council allows us to help our school and our community in fun and creative ways.

Haunted High School has been a very popular event for elementary kids from all around Galesburg ever since I was 3 years old and my mom made me a "one of a kind," pig costume. Games, activities, a haunted auditorium and, of course, candy, are some of the enchanting highlights of this special event.

It takes a lot of preparation for the event to run smoothly. For example, in order to have yummy treats for the witches, ghosts and pirates, one committee's responsibility is to contact area stores for donations of a bag or two of candy. Ms. Myers and Ms. Good are the faculty sponsors. They both have important roles in how our council operates, inspiring confidence so that we can in turn take on projects that entertain and make a difference.

One of the things I enjoy most about Haunted High School is how we have the chance to relive the days of our made-from-scratch or store-bought costumes by dressing up and handing out Skittles and Snickers bars to kids who look up to us, literally. Though there are many spectacular spook-houses and other fun frights for kids in and around the community, Haunted High School is a chance for the younger crowd to enjoy Halloween without getting so scared they can't still have a lot of fun.

Not only has the student council put a lot of hard work into making the high school extra ghoulish for this special night, but other organizations, such as Artte Clubbe, have made many contributions. With decorations and amazing murals, they make the night more special for all the little trick-or-treaters. All the time and energy will be worth it to see those excited eyes and grins of the kids when they walk, climb, crawl or flap, into the Haunted High School.

Now, where is that pig nose?

Finals Time - Fore!

OCTOBER 29

- -

WHEN I JOINED THE GALESBURG HIGH SCHOOL GIRLS GOLF TEAM, I improved my golf skills and got a chance to brush-up my vocabulary. I became acquainted with words like quadruple bogey, O.B. (out of bounds), penalty, provisional, and my personal favorite – fore! Although I did not play up to par my first year, I got to become friends with an awesome group of girls and take part in a great program.

Tuesday night was the banquet for both boys and girls golf teams at Lake Bracken Country Club. When our team captain and only senior Megan Pickrel talked about how proud she was of us as a team, I remembered all the fun times we shared together. I can think back to my first match and how nervous I was the whole day at school just knowing I was going to totally bomb on the course. I was so rattled I left one of my most important clubs, my putter, at home, even after my mom had reminded me to put it in my bag. Luckily though, my friend Jorden's dad pulled through for me by letting me borrow his putter for the match.

With shaken nerves and all, I ended up playing much better that day than I thought I would and felt relieved when our coach, Mrs. Gottenberg, told me I had done a good job. When I informed my teammates about my mishap, they all just laughed and began telling stories about the goofy things that happened to them in their first matches. Pretty soon we were all roaring with laughter.

This week, I will be faced with another new challenge: end-of-the-quarter finals. Normally I would be completely stressed out, but my positive experiences on the Streaks golf team have helped to lessen my fears when facing the unknown. By working hard on my studies as well as on the practice range, I believe I will be able to land good grades on my tests, like that fantastic tee shot from No. 7 at Bracken.

Halloween Reminds Her of Waning Youth

NOVEMBER 5

- -

ON HALLOWEEN NIGHT, I SAT ON THE STEPS OF MY FRONT PORCH handing out candy to all the cute little trick-or-treaters in their costumes. I started to realize that those adorable little ghouls and goblins used to be me. Not only was Halloween a reality check, but this past week there have been other gentle reminders that brought my age to attention.

On Tuesday, a three-week-old cough forced me to pay a visit to my pediatrician. While I sat with my mom in the waiting room, everything around me seemed to be different than I remembered. I noticed two toddlers playing with the old baby toys I used to have fun with, while the Disney movie "Toy Story" played on the elevated television.

Now, even my cafeteria experience is forcing me to jet into a galaxy unknown. In past years, my mom made my lunch, which always consisted of a sandwich, fruit and one of my grandma's homemade cookies. This year, I am faced with a new test: making healthy choices at lunch. At GHS, there are a lot of different places you can eat: the deli, salad bar, sub shop or the candy shop. Trips to the candy shop were a big hit in the beginning of the year but I quickly began to think that maybe eating a Snickers every day wasn't exactly following the Food Guide Pyramid.

Just this past week, I decided to change my eating habits by making more frequent visits to the deli for a nutritious salad and Sun Chips. Getting older is just another one of the many facts of life. There are good and bad points to the process.

But, I must say, when Doctor G. handed me a purple lollipop after my meningitis shot, she made me feel like a kid again.

Musical Selection Makes Sense at Last

NOVEMBER 12

- -

BACK IN LATE AUGUST, OUR BAND DIRECTOR, MR. B., EXPLAINED THE story behind "Braveheart," one of our marching selections.

The ballad about a man sacrificing his life for his country did not take on much meaning for me at the time. In the last few days, I have thought more about the story.

Last Thursday, Galesburg High School graduate and National Guard Sgt. 1st Class Kyle Wehrly was killed while laying his life on the line for his country in Iraq. Even though I never met Kyle, I feel a connection with him. For not only was he a graduate of GHS, but Kyle was also a member of the Galesburg High School Band. He played the tenor sax.

While walking through the halls this past week, I think of how Kyle must have walked through the same doors and sat in the same classrooms I am now occupying. Even my older brother, John, remembered Kyle as a referee at some of his varsity soccer games.

On Tuesday, all the band students were called down to the band room for an important meeting during advisory. Not knowing what was going on, we were all thinking of crazy things they may have wanted to talk to us about. Then Mr. Bredhemier explained to us that tonight was the homecoming for Kyle and we had been asked to play in his honor. Everyone looked around at each other and quietly understood that it would indeed be appropriate for us to play for him. The "Star Spangled Banner" and the theme from "Braveheart" were the selections chosen.

Now, when I think back to that day Mr. Bredhemier was trying to explain to us the peaceful and melodic way to play "Braveheart," I under-stand much better what he was saying. So, on Tuesday night, when we were standing side-by-side playing that beautiful and sad song for Kyle, it was the best we ever played it.

A Match Made in ...English Class?

NOVEMBER 19

OVER THE PAST COUPLE OF WEEKS, I HAVE TAKEN TESTS ON MY TYPing speed and accuracy, my ability to solve algebraic equations, and which guys I'm most compatible with at Galesburg High School.

Whoa, Nelly! What's wrong with this picture?

Last Tuesday, our advisory teacher, Ms. Hinman, presented us with a pop quiz. However, it was not a test of our grammar and punctuation, but a survey to detect who we were most compatible with at GHS. Immediately, the room was filled with high-pitched giggles from the girls and "oh great" groans from the guys. I actually thought it would be pretty interesting and possibly fun to discover who could be my potential "Knight in Shining Armor!"

I then began to wonder, could it be that super cute varsity football player? Or maybe even the kid in typing class who always fires spitballs my way? Or, heaven forbid, a male version of Jane Simkins. But once I started reading the questions, I realized some of them were pretty off-the-wall.

Here's a sample:

When you go out, do you wear - A. T-shirts and jeans, B. Saggy baggy clothes, or C. Nice clothes?

Even one of the boys in my class noticed the odd queries. "So, they're gonna base who I'm most compatible with by whether I prefer McDonald's or Burger King?" he sarcastically inquired.

Once we finished up our questions Ms. Hinman announced it would take four weeks for the results to arrive and, if you wanted them, they cost $2. I'm thinking it may be money well spent. Not only will this test tell me who I share qualities with, but it will also inform me of other students who might be good to get to know better.

But the real answer I'm anxious to know is: Am I suited for a frog or a potential Prince Charming?

RRRrrribit!

Special Thanks to Staff Behind the Scenes

NOVEMBER 26

- -

ONCE AGAIN, IT'S TIME TO STUFF THE TURKEY, VISIT WITH RELATIVES, and let your belt out another notch after filling up on Thanksgiving dinner.

Not only is this holiday about feasting on great food and chatting it up with family, it's a chance to give thanks for the obvious and not-so-obvious blessings in our lives that we often take for granted.

When walking from class to class in Galesburg High School this week, I have noticed that for a school full of teenagers, the hallways are sparkling clean. Thanks to our custodians, the treads on my Nikes have stayed gum-free and my nostrils have not been held prisoner by those strange smells coming from the boys' locker room.

If I asked any student at GHS what their favorite part of the school day was, they most likely wouldn't hesitate to say "lunch." The great thing about lunch is not just the yummy food, but the smiling faces you see as you slide your card through the scanner. Thanks to the incredible cooks at GHS, I'll never get that weak feeling during last-hour class or be freaked out about the surprise in the "meat loaf surprise."

As I begin to think of my future, I become overwhelmed about how I will be able to accomplish my dreams. How will I ever know what classes to take, when to prepare for the ACT test, or what colleges have the best boy-to-girl ratio? The wonderful advisers at Galesburg High School are there to point us in the right direction and help us to think of ways to achieve our goals, whether it be to ace a science test or get accepted to our favorite college.

Fortunately, I have not had an opportunity to visit the school nurse, but it is good to know that she is there if I were to be hit in the back of the head by a clumsy trombone player or get pummeled by a pickleball in P.E.

Without this cast of behind the scenes supporters, life at GHS would be like the Bubblicious gum on my shoe - blue, stuck, scary and going nowhere.

Express Yourself to a T

DECEMBER 3

SOME SAY THE WAY A PERSON DRESSES TELLS A LOT ABOUT THE INDI-vidual, but these days at Galesburg High School students are taking the statement to a new level.

The plain white cotton T-shirt of my parents' generation has been upstaged by the designer top of today. Whether it's a T-shirt with ABERCROMBIE, AC/DC with the lightning bolt, or my favorite, the St. Louis Cardinal perched on the baseball bat, the artwork on the front is the first impression given off by the wearer.

Though the walking billboards convey a certain attitude, they can be misleading. Yesterday I passed a girl with a shirt that had a smiley face on it, yet the words "turn that frown upside down" would have been more fitting.

Some of my peers demonstrate their school or team spirit by designing shirts with catchy little quotes on the back, such as "Swimmers are like tea-bags, you never know how strong they are until you put them in water." The volleyball team conveys its work ethic with the words "It's not the hours you put in, but what you put into the hours." And don't for-get those outgoing youngsters who have the guts to wear shirts that say "Brat" or "Little Devil" on them.

I've also come across a few shirts that got me laughing. For exam-ple, a guy in my algebra class once wore a shirt that gave hilarious tips on "How to get a date." Seemingly, every event has a historical record cap-tured on a T-shirt from the homecoming theme "Cruisin' the Caribbean" to the latest trip to Redbird Arena by the girls basketball team.

Sometimes color alone is powerful enough. As I enter John Thiel Gymnasium, the gold glow from the student section creates a strong message as well. In that case, the T-shirt is no longer an individual fashion statement, but serves as the ultimate display of school spirit.

Tomorrow morning as I open up my overflowing drawer of tees I will pause and ask, "How will I express myself today?"

Hey, is that my "I Love Nerds" shirt calling?

Shopping? Do the Math

DECEMBER 10

- -

ALGEBRA: THE BRANCH OF MATHEMATICS THAT DEALS WITH GENERAL statements of relations, utilizing letters and symbols to represent specific numbers and values, etc. So says the Random House College Dictionary. And I need to know about algebra, why?

This challenge was recently proposed by one of my fellow class-mates, we'll call him Henry, to my Algebra I teacher, Ms. Putney. Even though I thought Henry was just saying this to get a rise out of the teacher, I had to think to myself, maybe he's got a point there. I guess if I were heading into the field of architecture or engineering, I would need to obtain some knowledge of algebra. As neither of these careers "light my fire," I pondered the potential opportunities of using equations such as "y = mx + b" in my, as well as Henry's, everyday life.

I pictured Henry and his girlfriend in his tricked-out Mustang head-ing for a nice rendezvous at the Olive Garden in Peoria. Henry, having not paid attention in Algebra when Ms. Putney taught the class how to solve for "x" in simplified equations, figures 4 gallons of gas will make the trip. Using the formula d = gm, where d is the distance, g is the gallons of gas in the tank, and m is the miles per gallon used by a tricked-out Mustang, Henry would have known that 4 gallons of gas burned at the rate of 15 miles per gallon would get him and his girlfriend about 60 miles, leaving them stranded near the Kickapoo exit on the way home.

I also found algebra to be a big help in my life when I went shop-ping the other day in Peoria. There was one really adorable shirt that I "just had to have," but when I checked out the tag, it was a little pricey. Fortunately, my mother came to the rescue with a 25 percent off coupon. Now, I thought to myself, what form of algebra would I use to figure out how much this shirt costs? I soon remembered that you must convert the percentage to a decimal, multiply that number by the cost, and then subtract the result from the original price. The wonders of algebra put that shirt right in line with my limited budget and I even had enough left for a single scoop of rainbow sherbet.

It seems to me that no matter who you are or what you do, your grasp of algebra is enough to make or break your day. So, if "y" is equal to you, while "m" equals life, and "x" represents algebra, then y + m − x = Henry.

'Morp' Dance at GHS a Show of Respect

DECEMBER 17

A FEW WEEKS AGO, STUDENT COUNCIL PRESIDENT LAUREN MCCLURE announced that GHS was going to help out Kyle Wehrly's family by raising money to go toward an education fund for his daughter, Kylee.

There was a catch, though. We had to come up with a way to get the whole school involved and bring in money at the same time. That was when Lauren suggested we have a school dance, called "Morp." At first, we were all a little hesitant, figuring students would not be too excited to spend their Friday night at an event that sounded like something that was left in the microwave too long. Yet, once we were told what this extravaganza entailed our whole perspectives changed. It turns out that Morp not only spells prom backwards, but it is basically everything about prom turned upside down.

For instance, instead of guys and gals getting all "spiffed" up, sometimes the girls will dress as guys and the guys as girls which sounds pretty scary, but hilarious if you think about it. Of course, if a person did not feel like dressing up in their brother's baggy gym shorts or their sister's frilly skirt, they could always come casual. Another great thing about this fund-raiser is that you are not expected to go out and blow your snow shoveling money on a nice dinner for you and your date. Looks like Steak 'N' Shake and McDonald's are going to be hoppin' places Friday night!

Though all these positives are fantastic reasons to attend Morp, one stands out among them all, which is the whole point of holding this dance. Kyle Wehrly gave his life for our country. This dance will be a great way for Galesburg High School to thank him and his family for all they have sacrificed for us. So, as students gather to "boogie down" on Dec. 16, and donate their $4 at the door, they will be paying not only their admission fee, but their respects.

Ahhh-choing Through Christmas Break

DECEMBER 23

TODAY MARKS THE FIRST DAY OF WINTER AS WELL AS THE BEGINNING of Holiday Break for all schools in District 205. The shortest day of the calendar year coincides with a shortened day for Galesburg students. Normally, this would find me skipping joyously through the hallways at the jingle of the early dismissal bell. Visions of a Chevy Chase Christmas Vacation would be dancing in my head. Unfortunately, I am dealing with visions of hot tea and salt water gargling instead of dancing sugar plums. I have been bitten by the "common cold bug." I think a steady crawl through the halls will be adequate.

Yet, sore throat and all, I am determined to make these school-less 14 days the best I possibly can. To me, making snow angels, drinking hot chocolate, and throwing snowballs at my big brother, no matter how mad he may get, has always put me in the winter spirit.

Some of my friends also have little traditions of their own that fill their hearts with holiday memories. For instance, every Christmas my friend, Emily, helps her mom make beautiful glass ball ornaments for their tree. Another one of my classmates, Emma, is flying south with her family to her grandparents' house to celebrate Hanukkah. When she told me that she would be in one of the warmest states in America, I'll admit to becoming a tad green with envy. Or is that my post nasal drip talking?

Not only does winter bring close-to-home memories, but it also brings loved ones we haven't seen in a while. Recently, on television, there have been little clips of soldiers based in places all over the world sending their love and holiday wishes to friends and family waiting back home.

This year, instead of waiting up to hear Santa's sleigh bells, I will be looking for the headlights on my brother John's red Monte Carlo pulling into the driveway, completing a long drive from college in St. Paul, Minnesota.

I am also looking forward to catching up with one of my good friends, Sarah, who moved to Morton the summer following our seventh-grade year. All in all, winter is always at the top of my list of favorite seasons, because it is a time for revisiting old traditions and making new memories with the ones you care for. And this year, Rudolph, with his nose so bright, will have nothing on me... ahhh-choo!

2006 Hereby Dedicated to Lesser-Known Clubs

JANUARY 7

- -

5, 4, 3, 2, 1, HAPPY NEW YEAR!

With 2006 well on its way, resolutions have already been made and broken. Personally, I like to refer to resolutions as covenants of personal amendments, or "CPAs" for short. Since the days of the one-room schoolhouse, students have been making personal promises to themselves to improve their lives at the hanging of every new calendar.

This year, I decided to jump on the bandwagon of CPAs when I saw a headline on the six o'clock news explaining how bad pop is for the human body. Images of nasty dental work soon ran across my mind and jump-started my decision of giving up soda for an entire year, even my beloved Vanilla Coke. As I explained this to my table during C Lunch, they all kind of gave me that weird look someone gives you when you tell them you ate a worm during P.E. However, many reacted in a different way - by throwing some of their CPAs into the hat.

For instance, one of my friends said she would be ridding her taste buds of sweets for all 365 days. Also added to the "list of sacrifice" were goals to eat less sugar, exercise more and study harder. And then there is the most popular CPA at Galesburg High School, one that most students would gladly forfeit - giving up homework! Another CPA I have planned for this semester involves supporting the less visible clubs and activities at GHS.

Maybe I'll discover the subtle difference between a bowling pin and a wrestling pin by cheering on these less famous, yet equally talented Streak athletes who like to knock things down. Or, perhaps I can discover what crazy or "mad" lab experiments are being cooked up by the Science Club. So, here's to a new year of non-carbonated drinks, hitting the books harder and rooting for those uncelebrated brainiacs in Math Club or Scholastic Bowl. "GO MATHLETES!"

Finding Mr. Right Not a Lesson in Love
JANUARY 14

- -

WHILE SITTING IN CLASS WAITING FOR MY ENGLISH TEACHER TO DIS-tribute the final exams, I began to think about the last test I was given back, my compatibility quiz.

Earlier this week, I read a sign posted on the wall stating that the matches for the compatibility test were finally in. I instantly began going over my mental "dream list," contemplating whether that "Prince Charming" of mine would be at the top. All through fourth block, I continued to wonder about my other compatibles until the final bell rang. Yes! It was finally the moment of truth. Would I be destined to ride off into the sunset with Mr. Right, or the not-so-appealing Spitball Boy?

Waiting in line for the results seemed to last an eternity. Finally, the envelope was handed to me. It was white with lots of red hearts and tiny Cupids all over it. On the front, there was a little paragraph explaining how the results were "just for fun" and were not the answers to your love life. With trembling hands, I slowly ripped apart the envelope across the dashed lines and unfolded the piece of paper. My eyes were like fingers typing across a keyboard, hitting every name and its rank carefully one by one.

After reading the group of freshman guys who shared the same qualities with me, and girls who would make good friends, I found some names that surprised and some I would have chosen myself. Now, it was time for the upperclassmen (sophomores, juniors and seniors), and my heart began beating like crazy. Once again, my eyes ran as if they were at a track meet sprinting across each name, hurdling over to the next line. My eyes came to a screeching halt when the name Harry Potter popped up in bold black letters. At this, I laughed so hard that the boy next to me was in a state of shock, probably hoping it wasn't his name I was chuckling at.

Toward the end of the list were titles that read "Least Compatible" and "Random Compatible" which I glanced over a little but didn't worry too much about. When I finished reading, then re-reading the list, I soon became curious as to what lucky fellow had me as his perfect match. However, before I could get too deep in thought on that subject, I noticed the Web site that created the quiz was called ComputerFun.com. That's all it was, "Computer fun," I told myself, not a Ouija board or crystal ball that predicted my future. Although the test was made to show who I would get along with best, it also taught me something completely different. Whether it's the captain of the football team, the first-chair trumpet in band, or even Spitball Boy, matches can be found everywhere. Who knows? Maybe the next time I get a wad of paper thrown at me, I'll fire one right back.

Semester Heralds Changing Face of School

JANUARY 21

- -

CHANGE.

Some look forward to it, while others dread even the thought of it. With the first half of the school year under our belts, Tuesday kicked off the start of second semester at Galesburg High School, and quite frankly, it feels a bit uncomfortable.

Last semester, my daily routine at school started upstairs at typing, downstairs to English, a pit stop at Algebra 1A, C lunch with my friends. I finished the day blasting my bassoon in band.

Since the beginning of school on Tuesday, I no longer start my day flexing my keyboarding fingers. Instead, I'm stretching my mind with history facts. As changes are made to my schedule, so are the faces I see every day as I walk through the halls and sit down at lunch. Although I enjoy meeting new people, there is a part of me that misses my old crowd of buddies and the security of seeing them every day. Even something as simple as being able to depend on my friend, Katie, to always finish my chips, is a change I would rather not do without.

Changes are not only taking place in the school building, but also in my everyday life. For instance, the unfortunate event of my dog chewing up my backpack has forced me to switch to a brand new, grown-up, unfamiliar book bag. My brother returning to college on Saturday will change the amount of cereal in the cabinet and the volume of laughter in our home.

Even Mother Nature is experiencing some gradual changes as the sun is staying out a bit longer each day. Whether it's the comforting tapping of the keyboard, the unspoken friendship at the lunch table, or a torn-up backpack, change is a healthy and necessary part of life.

Better yet, inspiration to change is found in the words of Martin Luther King Jr:

"The soft-minded man always fears change. He feels security in the status quo, and he has an almost morbid fear of the new. For him, the greatest pain is the pain of a new idea."

Phew! Smells Like Spring at GHS

JANUARY 28

- -

EVERY MONDAY, WEDNESDAY AND FRIDAY AFTER THE FINAL BELL rings, I grab my backpack and bulky winter coat and head off to the girls' locker room to suit up for soccer conditioning. The calendar may say January, but spring is definitely in the air at Galesburg High School.

Since the weather outside is frightful, athletes can be found training in the hallways, balconies, and weight room, each preparing for his or her favorite athletic endeavor. For instance, instead of swinging for a home run at Jim Sundberg Field, the baseball team is "chopping wood" in the batting cages of Thiel Gymnasium.

The track team also has been getting in tip-top shape by running laps around the second floor square and cycling through other various exercises. It is motivating to see so many kids moving around and getting active. On the other hand, the atmosphere can be, well, less than inspirational. Just the other day, I innocently waltzed into the weight room without realizing the brutal attack of "B.O." that was to greet me at the door - Phew! I did manage to persevere through the layer of odor, however, long enough to pump some iron and even run a little on the treadmill.

After being in the weight room a number of times, I have noticed that I am a little on the weaker side compared to my fellow body-builders and have since figured out a little trick that sizes me up a bit. When I am done using a weight machine, I take the pin out of plate 4 and discreetly move it to 7. As the next person comes to the machine, they are amazed at what this girl can lift! Even if it seems that everywhere I turn someone is either jumping rope, tossing a medicine ball or lifting weights, athletes aren't the only ones prepping for competition.

The GHS color guard has been having practices for winter guard after school in front of the cafeteria which will give them a head start come fall marching band season. Project Graduation meetings also are under way as volunteers begin planning for a great senior celebration at the end of the year. So, despite the bad smells and sweaty locker rooms, the anticipation of an early spring when the doors of GHS will burst open with bottled-up energy spilling out onto the fields, tracks and ball diamonds, gives inspiration to the perspiration of the January blues.

GHS Lovin' The Music in Coming Week

FEBRUARY 4

- -

THE HALLS ARE ALIVE WITH THE SOUND OF MUSIC! FROM THE much-anticipated band festivities to the student council agenda, February is a month for rhythms and melodies here at Galesburg High School. This Sunday, the annual District 205 band concert will be held in the GHS auditorium at 2 p.m. This exciting festival highlights the talents of all the GHS concert bands as well as Churchill and Lombard junior high musicians. The grand finale will feature a spectacular presentation of all the bands playing in unison a most fitting tune - "Bandorama."

With so many musicians performing this final number, band members will be forced to take positions in the aisles around the auditorium. Audience members will need to be on the lookout for sliding trombonists and jabbing flautists. However, it is not just the music departments that are preparing for a symphony of sound. On Wednesday at 6:30 p.m., the auditorium will be jam-packed with student and community groupies for the annual Sweetheart Swirl Battle of the Bands. This school-sponsored jam session is an opportunity for passionate rockers and rollers at GHS to strut their stuff in front of their peers. I will be supporting and cheering on my friend Emily as she performs with her bodacious band, Yourself in the Process.

The place will be filled with posters declaring a beloved band while cell phones will illuminate the air in a colorful show of support for a favorite sound. Melodies were also being sung in Lecture Room B Tuesday morning at the student council meeting. "A Romance in France" is the theme for Swirl this year and one of the student council's tasks was coming up with the theme song for the dance. Girls sat straight up in their chairs with eyes all aglow as the guys pulled their hats over their faces when it was time to throw out ideas. With the chalkboard covered in song titles, the members voted and chose "L.O.V.E." to be played as the Swirl melody.

As this song proclaims: "L" is for the way you look at me, "O" is for the only one I see. "V" is very, very, extraordinary, and "E" is even more than you adore. So, the way I see it, everyone should Look at attending a one and Only, Very, very, extraordinary music event at GHS that is Even more fun than renting the Julie Andrews film.

All Costs Aside, Swirl Worth a Whirl

FEBRUARY 11

CHA-CHING! CHA-CHING!

These are the sounds heard throughout GHS this week as students begin to learn not only the value of education, but of a dollar. With the anticipation of Saturday's turn-about dance, formally known as "Sweetheart Swirl," students have been raiding their piggy banks, hoping to create a night to remember. For most guys, preparations for Swirl are simple, but not very cheap. Renting a standard tux ($60), picking up the corsage ($20), gas and a fresh wax job on the Mustang ($20), Tic-Tacs and deodorant ($4).

Girls on the other hand are usually a bit of a different story. Finding the perfect dress ($100), hairdo ($30), dinner ($20), getting all dolled up without looking like Bozo the Clown's twin sister ($25).

For those with dates, there is the fun of coordinating the color scheme of the tux, the dress, the corsage, and the boutonniere. After adding in the tickets ($10) and the obligatory photo shoot at the dance ($15), the event can become a tidy investment. The good news is that there exist many shortcuts to having an equally, maybe even better, Swirl experience using the resources right inside your classroom.

For instance, instead of ordering a flower or corsage for your date, just head on over to horticulture class and grow your own carnations! Instead of taking out a mortgage on the house to pay for a dress or tux, bop on over to home economics and sew yourself one. Say goodbye to expensive dinner reservations and cook up your own filet mignon in Cooking 101. When it comes to buying that perfect shade of red for your blush, try mixing up a personal concoction in chemistry class.

Finding a friend to share the gas and wax money by carpooling can help ease the budget. I have decided to save some cash myself by borrowing a dress from my cousin and doing my own makeup and nails. Receipts or no receipts, Swirl is all about having a good time and making great memories with friends. Priceless!

Life was Simpler During Silas Days

FEBRUARY 18

I'M TIRED. SOMEWHERE BETWEEN HURLING MYSELF OUT OF THE cozy comfort of "Dreamland" and arriving in the nick of time for the first bell at Ms. Townsell's U.S. Government class, I think back to the days when life was simple.

In my early years of education, school mornings were a breeze: Wake up, throw on my favorite purple polka dot jumper, run a comb through my bed head hair, and out the door I went with a chocolate milk-mustached smile to greet Mrs. Renfroe at Silas.

However, once I hit the stage where I began to realize the Pebbles Flintstone hairdo was out of style, and that stripes and polka dots didn't match, school mornings turned into a race against time:

6:15 a.m. - please, no, don't say it, Dad. "Time to get up."

6:18 - again ... "Jane, are you up?" hmmmph. "All right, already."

6:21 - who turned the thermostat down to 40?

6:22 - shower knob all the way to the right.

6:23 - conscious once again.

6:31 - Colgate away Mr. Morning Breath.

6:33 - first attempt at today's hairdo.

6:40 - morning exercise program of stretching out those freshly dried jeans with a few knee raises.

6:45 - second attempt at today's 'do.

6:50 - hunt down my algebra homework.

7:01 - hair is not happening!

7:05 - "Jane, you gotta eat something."

7:09 - what did Boomer do with my shoe?

7:13 - catch that bagel, "nice throw, Mom."

7:17 - forget it, it's another ponytail day.

7:20 - "they're here - got the cellphone, backpack, bassoon, ID, gym bag, lunch money? You have to wear a coat!"

7:22 - "Hey, Emily - nice ponytail."

7:32 - "thanks for the ride, Andrew."

7:34 - dodge drowsy drivers in parking lot.

7:43 - "Good morning, Ms. Townsell."

7:46 - "where's your other shoe, Jane?"

7:46:07 - I'm tired.

Genetics Shape Our Faces, Not Our Futures

FEBRUARY 25

- -

ALL MY LIFE I HAVE BEEN TOLD I HAVE MY FATHER'S SMILE AND MY mother's nose. However, it was not until this week that I learned the scientific explanation for these quirky traits.

This Monday in biology, Ms. Gehring surprised us by assigning a chapter on genes. I soon began to question the biological relevance of flared-leg Levis. But as we discussed topics in genetics like dominant and recessive traits, self and cross-pollination and the difference between homozygous and heterozygous genes, I began to understand the real reasons for orthodontists and plastic surgeons.

From the time I was able to eat solid foods until sixth grade, I grinned and bared a gap-toothed smile that would give even Mike Tyson a run for his money. My dad and I always played the Dennis the Menace joke where you put a Chicklet in your gap and carefully smile while trying to contain your laughter. My mother thought this trademark smile was so cute when I was about 8, she entered me in a competition for the "It Girl" for Gap Clothing. I received a nice Gap ball cap with a letter confirming how "cute" I was. No contract, though.

I noticed at the time people were also calling our dog Roscoe cute, and he had all his teeth. By sixth grade my gap went from being cute to the often-asked question, "Did you lose a tooth?" - so annoying. So, with the help of Dr. Joe and his pair of metallic train tracks, 16 months later I graduated to a silver monorail used to keep my new chompers in place.

My parents' genes also have determined the shape of my nose, but it will be up to me to determine the shape of my future. A little part of me hopes the future includes a pack of Chicklets.

High School Lockers Lead Lives of Their Own

MARCH 4

THEY ARE OUR FRIENDS.

We throw our books in them, slam them when we are mad, or don't use them at all. Lockers are undersized and overstuffed, and mostly unappreciated. But without their service, we students would be lugging our notebooks, gym clothes, and half-eaten lunches around GHS like teenage pack mules. Though all lockers may be painted with the same dark brown color, it's how they look on the inside that makes them unique.

Many of my friends for example, decorate their lockers according to their personalities and hobbies. Pictures of friends and family, athletic and academic ribbons, as well as memos for upcoming events are stuck to, piled in, framed on, or forever entombed in the bottom of these metallic vaults. I have also learned that lockers can store history such as past owners, past loves, and ... dun, dun, DUN ... past enemies.

Some of my pals are like pack rats jamming everything from graded tests to old Gatorade bottles in their locker. Just yesterday, my friends and I were startled by our classmate Matt's locker as it spilled its contents of baseballs, bats and other athletic equipment into the hallway. Students even use the inside of their lockers as personal beauty salons for those quick touch-ups after a sweaty game of dodgeball.

In contrast, there is the super-organized student with her books neatly placed in alphabetical order, her Papermate pencils separate from her Bic pens, her class schedule neatly framed on the inside of the door. There are also many instances of students sharing lockers with their best buds. This friendly practice can save a lot of time and footwear if the friend has a convenient location near that class of yours at the far end of the building but can make it confusing at times to know whose bio book is whose.

My friend Emily, for instance, is nice enough to let me be her locker-mate. There have been many times we have taken each other's algebra book or agenda and did not realize it until we got to class. Occasionally and sadly, an orphaned locker sits unused, containing nothing but stale high school air trapped inside from a previous year.

Trashed or organized, shared or unused, a GHS locker is a reflection of the person spinning its three-number combination each day. Like the countless combinations of left-right-left numbers, each year brings the promise of a different personality into the life cycle of one of our dearest high school friends.

Chemistry Class Perfect Topping for 'Pi Day'

MARCH 11

- -

I'D LIKE THE REVOLUTIONARY WAR FOR $200 PLEASE, MS. TOWNSELL!

Instead of sticking to daily worksheets and repetitive note-taking, teachers at GHS have discovered creative techniques that make learning both fun and educational. For instance, as I walked into biology class on Monday, Ms. Gehring announced that we would be starting a new chapter on DNA replication. Without hesitation, I grabbed my notebook and pencil and waited for her to pull up a long list of notes on the overhead. I was delightfully surprised, however, when Ms. G whipped out a clear container of Driscoll strawberries and informed us that we would be extracting "DNA" from their cells. Inventive instruction has also made its mark in the mystical realm of Greek mythology.

By allowing each student to search his or her own imagination, my English teacher, Ms. Hinman, had each of us creating our own mythical adventures. Even typing class is becoming more exciting. Students' fingers become their favorite NASCAR drivers as they are encouraged to keyboard-race the computer to reach the top level of the game.

And Ms. Schulz has declared it "Pi-Day" next Tuesday in Algebra, honoring March 14 (3.14). My fellow classmates and I get the chance to bring in circle-shaped snacks or real pie of edible diameter.

Popular games such as Battleship and Jeopardy also have been incorporated in my studies in U.S Government class. I never knew students could get so competitive with the 27 Amendments!

The band staff has made the conclusion of marching camp a thrill a minute with the oh-so-famous "Band Olympics." There's nothing like challenging the flute section to an attention stand-off on a hot and sweaty August evening. While there's still plenty of reading, writing and 'rithmetic in the classrooms at GHS, our teachers have built an enjoyable atmosphere that is open to using new ideas to learn the same old thing. I think I'll run down to the chemistry lab on Tuesday. I hear they are using liquid nitrogen or something to make ice cream. What a great topper for "Pi-Day!"

Finals are Coming, So How to Prepare?

MARCH 18

- -

BIOLOGY HAS NEVER BEEN MY BEST SUBJECT.

When I was 5, I thought all babies came from a big white bird with a hat that read "Stork" on it. In third grade, I thought my guinea pig was a boy and a week later it had babies. In junior high, I put two praying mantises in a cage planning to take them to class the next day for my big insect collection. To my shock, however, they ate each other.

Unfortunately, there's always that one subject that gives students a hard time. Whether it's graphing fractions in algebra, remembering dates in history, or even being timed in keyboarding, most of us have a bug-aboo in a particular area. But without being a bit of a challenge, school would lose much of its purpose and excitement.

Within the next two weeks, finals will come knockin' at the door of GHS, and knots are already beginning to form in the pit of my stom-ach. How should I study? What do I need to review? With whom should I study? With these and many more thought-provoking questions buzzing in my mind, I asked my fellow pupils how they're going about studying for the hour-long tests.

Most of my friends admitted they will probably end up cramming the night before ... go figure. On the other hand, some claimed they had already begun going over the notes and re-reading the chapters in their textbooks. A few smarties are even dismissing the idea of reviewing altogether. And, for those who might need a little extra help preparing, there are tutoring sessions after school where students having a certain strength in one subject can give pointers to other students having diffi-culties with the same class. Teachers also lend a helping hand by assisting students before or after school with their homework. Finally, the learning center is open for any student who needs a quiet place to concentrate.

Like biology, final exam week can be a daunting experience loom-ing ahead for many students. I am subscribing to the theory that what doesn't kill me will only make me stronger. I'm just hoping there won't be a praying mantis looking over my shoulder during my biology final.

Names Change but GHS Clubs Continue

MARCH 25

- -

GHS 1976 - PEP CLUB PROVIDED BUS MONEY FOR OUT-OF-TOWN sports games while the Student Action for Education raised money through Tootsie pop sales. GHS 2006 - Film Club held movie screenings for students after school and Stage Call performed "Bye Bye Birdie" at the end of the month.

Over the years, clubs and activities at GHS have changed with the times. Once popular groups like Radio Club and FHA, Future Homemakers of America, have been dropped and replaced with new activities such as Technology Education Club and Key Club. In the '70s, offbeat groups such as Program Action and Concern and the Girls Service League focused entirely on helping those less fortunate in the community. By remodeling old toys, singing Christmas Carols and visiting the elderly in nursing homes, they carried out their missions. While these groups are no longer around, service organizations like Key Club and C.A.R.E have taken up the cause.

As for Dr. Laura and Dr. Phil, GHS has its own rendition known as peer mediators. In the days of white belts and bell-bottoms, organizations like Creative Writing and Pasteur Society (Science Club) were for students wanting to expand their academics outside the classroom. Today, Math Club and Scholastic Bowl reflect the competitive nature of 21st century society. While many activities have changed over the years, a good many are still going. Student Council continues at GHS for students wishing to have a say in how the school functions. Artte Clubbe was an outlet for the right-brained student 30 years ago and still is today. Foreign Language clubs like German, Latin, Spanish and French have always been popular among students desiring to expand their linguistics.

In support of club-life is the ever-popular fund-raiser. Money-making routines have gone from the traditional bake sales and summer car washes to marketing sterling silver jewelry and bagging groceries at Econo Foods. All in all, what's great about clubs is that they give students a chance to participate in their favorite hobbies and, sometimes, help others along the way.

Road Trip Adds Up to Great Memories

APRIL 1

- -

ONE YELLOW SCHOOL BUS + ONE HIGH SCHOOL GIRLS SOCCER TEAM + one boom box = ROAD TRIP.

When Coaches Tim Redington and Jim Carrothers handed out the schedules for the spring 2006 soccer season, I was a little down to see that most of our games were away. However, once I stepped on the school bus early Saturday morning before our first game in Normal, my whole perspective changed.

Around 6:30 in the morning, I'm usually awake enough to understand and comprehend light conversation, but if someone threw a Nerf ball at me, it would most definitely bonk me in the face. So, when I arrived at the school, I was surprised to see so many wide-awake teenagers on this early cartoon morning.

Thanks, Java Station.

Peppy is the only word I could use to describe my teammates. After finding a cold pleather seat on the bus, I was immediately greeted by a camera flash right at my face followed by a trail of laughter from my two buddies, Caitlin and Lindsey. A little shocked at first, I quickly busted out laughing at the sight of my half-groggy, half-confused face on the 2-by-3-inch digital screen.

Laughter was in great supply, as it contagiously spread from one girl's funny story to another's telling of a side-splitting joke. With JV seated up front and varsity settled in the back, the hour and a half road trip was the perfect setting for team bonding.

As we bumped along the road to Normal Community, the JV girls began to share how nervous we were for our first game. Would we miss the ball on a PK kick? Would the other team outrun us? Or even worse, would there be no bathrooms at the field? Some varsity members did calm our fears, however, and told comical stories of years past when they were in our cleats.

Another high point of the trip was when one of our seniors, Kristin, broke out a boom box and started a karaoke solo to some hit songs on mixed CDs. Even though the old boom box couldn't play half the tunes, most everyone on the bus still showed off their vocals and sang without the music. An occasional glance up front would catch one of the coaches grinning and shaking his head as we all broke out in harmony together.

Though we may have cracked a few mirrors when we tried to reach the high notes, the whole team got a kick out of our incantations. In fact, the bus ride was so much fun that the JV almost forgot we fell to Normal 5-0 while the varsity claimed a 1-1 tie.

Speed bumps and all, it won't be the number of games we lost that stands out in the end, but the funny photos and musical memories we made on our road trip through high school.

From Sports to Fashion, Signs of Spring Abound

APRIL 8

- -

A NEW EPIDEMIC HAS TAKEN OVER AT GHS - SPRING FEVER. WITH spring break only a few days away, students are showing signs of great anticipation.

Already some of my fellow classmates are bubbling about their plans for the week off. One of my friends, David, is migrating to New Mexico with his family over the break. Meanwhile, I will be staying in town, or at least in Illinois and Iowa, with three soccer games coming up. Between matches, I am planning to re-evaluate my wardrobe. Wintry colors such as brown and gray have been cut out of the fashion scene for now as brighter colors such as lime green and tickle-me-pink are popping up in trends. There is nothing like a much-procrastinated dose of spring cleaning to put a damper on the fun of spring fever.

Beyond the the green grass and sprouting daffodils, there are plenty of sure-fire signs that April has arrived on West Fremont Street. Students are copping creative methods to get outside the stuffy halls and class-rooms. A classmate, Dan, suggested we make biology more of a firsthand experience with a back-to-nature class in the courtyard, while the outdoor living class is starting to hear the blue-gills jump at Lake Storey. There are other, more subtle signs of the season, many of which are worn in exotic head to toe fashion by the various sports combatants.

The bruised shins of the Girls soccer team, the eye-black on the faces of coach Gonzalez's baseball players, the wind-blown hair of the track guys and gals, and the strawberries sprouting on the knees of slid-ing Streaks softballers, are all can't-miss signals that spring has arrived at GHS. In addition, there is lots of activity each day on the west side of the school parking lot as workers are breaking the thawed ground. Next year, the much-traveled tennis team will be loving its new home-court advan-tage on this former vacant lot.

Spring break offers students and teachers a chance to take a breath, gather steam, and prepare for the home stretch (as Mr. Cheesman would say). Let the games begin!

Whatever's Found Not Likely to Be What You Lost

APRIL 15

- -

WRINKLY OLD GYM T-SHIRTS, A LEFT-HANDED MITTEN, GLASSES WITH only one lens, backpacks with broken zippers. Pretty much any and everything you could ever imagine, can be discovered in the Galesburg High School lost and found.

Except of course, exactly what you are trying to find.

This past week, I reached the ripe old age of 15. Magically, my memory disappeared faster than my birthday money. I started my week with losing not one, but two pairs of soccer cleats. The first pair I misplaced in East Moline, while the second pair I sadly left right outside Wicall Gym.

Luckily, my teammates Laura and Emma spared me the wrath-of-responsibility lecture and picked up my muddy footwear on their way out. Soccer cleats are not the only victims on my long list of misplaced items. Also included are prescription glasses, retainers, coats, library books and everything else under the sun. Forgetfulness runs in my family.

My brother John is the king of losing stuff. A few of the outstanding items on his list: class ring, jacket, baseball glove, car keys, shoes and two graphing calculators. On the bright side, most of the items on both of our lists have miraculously appeared after weeks, months, even years have passed.

Just last weekend my dad found three long-forgotten soccer balls that had been kicked under the deck in the back yard. Well, actually four, as I clumsily shot another one right back under the stairs - Goal!

I have also learned that when you borrow something that belongs to someone else, it's best to make sure you take good care of it. For instance, whenever I borrow a pair of my mom's earrings, I carelessly place them in some nook or cranny in the bottom of my purse or athletic bag. Then the next day, when my mom asks for her jewelry back, I end up spending up to an hour hunting down something the size of a Life Saver. If the earrings do not turn up, then I am the recipient of an all-expense-paid trip to Guilt Land for about a week.

My goal this weekend is to improve my skills of memory and focus. So, while everyone else is hunting for plastic eggs around Grandma Shirley's gazebo, I will be tracking down my black nylon jacket instead of yellow Peeps.

Emotional Week Like a Roller Coaster Ride

APRIL 22

- -

ROLLER COASTERS HAVE NEVER BEEN MY CUP OF TEA. WITH THEIR winding turns and fierce names like "The Tornado," "Screamin' Eagle," and "Ring of Fire," these amusement park attractions are meant for those with nerves of steel - not me.

This past week, I felt like I was thrown unwillingly onto a different kind of roller coaster called The Roller Coaster of Emotions. The ride began with a downhill jolt of sadness on Saturday when I learned my cousins from Iowa would not be able to make it to my grandma and grandpa's house for Easter weekend. However, a backyard pick-up game of Wiffle ball with my hometown cousins was just the cure for my bummed-out blues, especially when the girls beat the boys.

Just as I was at the height of my happiness, I experienced a loop-the-loop in my stomach as Monday morning announced that spring break was officially over, along with my dreamy days of sleeping in. Right as I was about to give up hope, however, a little ray of sunshine broke through the gloomy clouds, and I felt like I was coasting smoothly through the week. High test scores in one of my hardest classes, biology, gave me the hope that I could take control of my destiny. Unfortunately, the mention of mumps at GHS not only threatened my immune system, but my optimism for the next few days and made me hold on for dear life.

Just when I thought my week was a goner, both our JV and varsity teams were victorious over Peoria Christian on our home soccer field. There's nothing like a good ol' team huddle after a win to pump you up! But reality has a way of slapping you in the face in short order. My peak and valley ride took its deepest plunge as we learned that a member of our coach's family was ill. In comparison, my Roller Coaster of Emotions, so big in my mind on Tuesday, now seems - on Thursday - like a gentle turn on a 5-year-old's merry-go-round.

Job-Shadowing Shows Benefits of Suspenders

APRIL 29

- -

THEY DESIGN OUR STREETS AND PARKING LOTS, THEY KEEP US SAFE, they set and enforce our laws, they pay the bills, and most importantly, they keep our city running smoothly.

Wednesday, a group of U.S. government students, including myself, participated in City Government Day, an opportunity to learn about the people working at City Hall and the Public Safety Building. Our day started off with a warm welcome from Mayor Smith as well as Mrs. Carlton, Mr. Goddard and Mr. Parkin. In just the few minutes we spent with them, I began to feel like an expert on the inner-workings of our community. I never thought I would have to see the inside of a police station until we toured it and several other interesting places in the Public Safety Building. The dispatch room for instance, looked like a kiddie carnival with tons of colorful flashing lights and the dispatchers keeping busy on the phones and radios.

Following the tours, we stopped in Knox College's Lincoln Room for lunch which was sponsored by the Noon Rotary Club. After we were all stuffed with great food, we headed back over to City Hall to experience job shadowing with staff members. My group stayed with the firefighters while some of my other friends went with engineers, secretaries or police. Whenever I heard the phrase "job shadowing," I always imagined myself quietly lurking around someone while they went about their day.

I was proven wrong, however, when I chose to shadow the firefighters. First off, we actually got into turnout gear: air tanks and masks, huge black boots, heavy yellow coats and pants and all. I immediately imagined my mom trying to get the smoky scent out of my khakis.

Next up, we were given walkie talkies and individual roles such as the Chief, the rescue squad and the attack team. Childhood memories of the Power Rangers flashed through my mind. We were then given a mission to "rescue" someone from the "flaming" house upstairs. Even though we knew it was all fake, we dragged a heavy hose up three flights of stairs in that "burning" building and saved the "victim" as if it were a real fire. My search buddy Jenna found him with a special see-in-the-dark camera.

Toward the end of the tour, it was fun to see my classmates Blake and Caleb proudly wearing the bright red, plastic fire helmets and feeling like 6-year-olds again. Some of my friends told funny stories of how their job-shadowing went. My friend, Kristin, described the awkward looks people gave her as she rode in the back of a police car through town. It was a fun, educational and hard-working day, which left me with one thought: Thank goodness for those red suspenders!

End-Of-Year Dash Cause for a Breather

MAY 6

- -

THIS WEEK, I FEEL AS THOUGH I'M BACK IN SIXTH-GRADE TRACK RUNning the 1600 meter.

Four laps around the track trying to keep on the heels of the person in front of me while saving enough energy for the big kick at the end. As the conclusion of my freshman year approaches, my first lap at GHS has become a quarter-mile race in itself. Having rounded the last turn and seeing the finish line ahead, I am more than anxious for the breather of summer vacation.

However, there is still that last, most important sprint of the fourth term. On the plus side, the last 50 yards involves a run of banquet-hopping. While I'm not sure what or where the word "banquet" comes from, it sounds French and worth tons of Scrabble points. These end-of-the-season hurrahs provide students a chance to dress up in something other than a sweaty, grass-stained uniform, eats lots of fabulous food at someone else's expense, and hear coaches, who have been motivating athletes all year, say wonderful things about their players. They are fun and exciting. I will be attending the Girls soccer banquet, the student council banquet, and the annual band banquet.

Speaking of band, the Big Band Dip at GHS on May 12 also is on the home stretch. Great music, homemade pie and ice cream, good ol' fashioned swing dancing, and a "high-stakes" raffle. Sounds like heaven, right? While the high school jazz band is tuning up their instruments for the "dip," other GHS musicians are stringing their basses and oiling their valves in readiness for the annual spring concerts. The wind symphony will team up with the eighth-graders on Sunday and my own concert band will play with the symphonic band on Tuesday. All the performances are at good ol' GHS.

Just thinking about all the fun activities coming up on my final sprint is giving me a sideache and shin splints. Where's that second wind? I'm gonna need it.

Nothing to Fear in The Big House

MAY 13

- -

THIS WEEK I WOULD LIKE TO WELCOME THE UPCOMING FRESHMEN with a little preview of what to expect once they reach "The Big House."

Before entering my ninth-grade year, I heard a great many horror stories about life at GHS. Many of those tall tales revolved around getting lost on your first day. I quickly came to realize, however, that you do not need a compass or a global positioning system to find your classes. After all, the building has only two levels and is pretty much a square of hallways bounded on four sides by the office, auditorium, gymnasium and learning center.

The square has three arms sticking out from it where they put all the noisy activities. The left arm is the hall for Band and Chorus, the right arm is the hall for weird science projects, and the neck in the middle above the gym is for fun stuff like woodworking, welding and working on cars. Even if I had difficulties discovering a classroom, the teachers were very approachable and were happy to point me in the right direction.

Other reassuring facts - there's no such thing as a "swirly" and it's nearly impossible to stuff someone in a locker. Also, upperclassmen do not have fangs or piercing red eyes. In fact, most juniors and seniors are very welcoming and refer to freshmen as "oh-so-cute," rather than annoying pests.

Here are a few tips on how to make your high school experience enjoyable. The biggest way to meet new people is through extracurricular activities. Whether it be in marching band, Key Club, student council, cross country or Stage Call, getting involved in your school is a huge advantage in making new friends. School functions such as pep rallies, dances and big athletic events are also a great opportunity to mingle with new crowds even if you are a bit shy. When it comes to lunch, try out a new line or menu item each day just to mix it up a bit. For those less adventurous, the pizza and chicken sandwich are a safe bet, while a yogurt will always hit the spot.

After a few days or weeks, The Big House on West Fremont will seem much smaller, the people more familiar, and the routine more, well, routine. Piece of cake!

Pull Up a Slab and Do the Horizontal Flop

MAY 20

- -

YOU WOULD THINK THAT WITH A TWO-STORY SCHOOL FULL OF CHAIRS there would be no reason for 15 students to cram together on top of a 9-foot heater. When it comes to my fellow GHS classmates and me, we often find ourselves congregating in the most unlikely places, even if our backsides get burned!

Each morning as I make my trek to U.S. Government Class, I notice the same trio of guys lounging on the main hallway window sill. Every time I see the "three amigos," as I like to call them, I wonder what is so comfy or even attractive about a hard, dusty slab of granite. Not to mention the blinding early morning sun that blasts through the open courtyard and reflects off the 11-by-11-foot glass window.

Even at lunch, students are leaving the good 'ol round tables and long benches empty for a spot on the cold, harsh tile floor underneath the stairs. I find myself thinking that maybe that day I was absent they announced sitting at tables was no longer what the "cool kids" were doing. Some band students even prefer carpeted steps to chairs with backs as they trill their flutes.

Maybe it's the fireplace-like warmth the heaters give off in the winter that attracts a chilled teenager or the refreshing coolness of the granite slab on a stuffy August day. Perhaps it's all about that natural teenage instinct to rebel, be different, turn a complete 180 degrees from everyone else. Or maybe it's a reaction from all the years in elementary school when we used to sit on those hard wooden "chesks," you remember, the ones with the chair attached to the desk. You couldn't sit "in" one of those without being in a studious frame of mind.

Maybe the obvious answer is that with today's kids spending so much of our time in class, in automobiles, or in front of TVs and computers, we have become accustomed to sitting. We will plop down anywhere, anytime. Whatever the reason, there is a definite trend at GHS toward occupying anything horizontal, whenever possible.

Time to end this week's journal entry - got to get in that daily workout on my stationary bike.

Only One Known Cure for Dreaded Senioritis

MAY 27

- -

SENIORITIS.

Symptoms may include drowsiness, an unexplained giddiness, loss of ability to pay attention in class, and random acts of hysteria. This temporary condition typically appears just after spring break and develops into a full-blown epidemic by Memorial Day. It is most common among high school seniors and is spread from student to student by word of mouth. The only cure for senioritis is a cap, gown and diploma.

Today is the last day of attendance for the soon-to-be-grads at GHS and it seems as if senioritis has reached pandemic levels. Twelfth-graders everywhere are cruising down the halls, making pit stops at friends' lockers for the last time along the way. Another popular side effect that comes with senioritis is flashbacks. Class time becomes story time as seniors reminisce about their past high school years and good times shared with friends and classmates growing up in Galesburg.

Other signs of senioritis appeared around lunch time as students began choosing alternate dining locations with fellow classmates. With the weather being so nice lately, a couple of my friends, Alex and Luis, enjoyed their lunch break out in the courtyard instead of the highly populated cafeteria.

Given the right conditions, senioritis can be highly contagious, creeping into the bones of freshmen as well. This entire week, I have been spacing off during first hour (sorry, Mrs. Townsell, for missing part of your lecture on the criminal justice system) thinking about the "Senior Moments" I have experienced this year. I can remember my first day of golf practice when our senior captain Megan drove my friend Jorden and me to Subway, even though we were "wimpy little freshmen."

I can also think back to how excited my freshman friends and I were to be invited by senior soccer players Carlie and Kathy to join their indoor team during the winter months. Early morning student council meetings were always exciting with vice president Kristen pumping us all up for events such as Homecoming and Haunted High School.

Tomorrow, the halls will feel less crowded, there will be good food selections in the cafeteria, and finding a place to park in the morning will be a breeze. Why then do I feel so sad? Seniors, thanks for the memories. Hey, is that a gold tassel hanging from the flagpole?

Many Freshman Lessons Learned Out of Class

JUNE 3

REFLECTING ON MY FRESHMAN YEAR, I REALIZE THAT GHS HAS taught me many lessons, some beyond the textbook.

One fact I learned about myself this year is that I can to walk up and down jam-packed stairs while carrying three heavy textbooks, four folders, two notebooks, and one bulging pencil bag without dropping a single paper clip. I have also come to realize, the hard way, that its a good idea to make sure my alarm clock is set for 6 o'clock a.m rather than p.m.

Furthermore, compatibility tests are not reliable predictors for selecting future boyfriends, an area in which I have had the least opportunity for learning this year. Oh well. Athletics has taught me the importance of teamwork, practicing with intensity and focus, and the art of layering. As any soccer junkie can tell you, the temperature behind Gale School is always a minimum of 10 degrees colder than your back yard.

I also discovered that art class is a great way to exercise my creativity and be rewarded for thinking outside the box. Participating in school activities encouraged me to meet new people and increased my connection to the school. There is nothing like dangling off the balcony rail while taping a black streamer for a dance to make a person feel a real physical, please-don't-let-me-fall kind of bond with the building.

Marching in August heat and humidity is hot. Bottom line. End of story. But the thrill of winning a band competition because of all that August preparation taught me that our band directors had a method to their madness.

Perhaps the most important lesson I have learned this year is that life is short and how important it is to live each day to its fullest, even if I didn't ace my math test or my eyes were closed in my school picture.

The final thing I have discovered is everyone needs a break now and then. So, as I replace my HP keyboard with SPF 15 sunblock, I will be signing off from my journal just for a while, until the leaves on the trees begin to change colors and it is time once again to walk up those GHS steps ... as a sophomore.

SOPHOMORE YEAR

No Time to Snooze, That's the Tardy Bell

AUGUST 26

- -

And.... we're back!

It's time for me to trade in my beach bag for a book bag, exchange my Lakeside summer pass for a Student ID and remind myself not to hit the "snooze" button on the alarm clock. The next time a bell sounds I won't be skipping for the ice cream man but scurrying to get to English class on time. Yes, indeed, the new school year is already knocking at my door and, surprisingly, I can hardly wait.

One of the things I look forward to most about the first day of school is how everything is brand new. Whether it's a notebook, classroom, an attitude or even a fresh No. 2 pencil, the idea of starting off with a "clean slate" gives me confidence for the upcoming year. As a sophomore, I will be given the chance to take a few courses I've never experienced. For instance, in my second block chemistry class I will be discovering what really makes those beakers bubble and what Fe represents in the Periodic Table.

I'm also eagerly anticipating that, officially, I'm no longer a "rookie." That's right, the torch of youth has been passed. Now that I am a seasoned veteran of GHS, I'll be expected to help find classrooms, open jammed lockers and most importantly welcome the class of 2010 to GHS.

Additionally, I'm thrilled for the return of weekends to their treasured status, especially those Friday nights when a home football game is on the schedule. What could be better than spending a cool summer night at Van Dyke Field with a big crowd cheering our team to victory as the horn section of the Marching Streaks blasts out "The Silver and the Gold" from across the field?

Yes, for the eleventh time in my life, school has begun. My spare time is no longer spare, my crossword puzzles will soon be replaced with chemistry formulas, and my leisurely breakfast will go from a slow bowl of Lucky Charms to a barely defrosted, out-the-door Eggo. I will once again be playing beat the clock to accomplish all the deadlines, homework assignments and activities while trying to keep my hair looking somewhat presentable. Bring it on!

New Year School Year Relatively Bump-Free

SEPTEMBER 2

PING! PING! THE PAINFUL SOUND OF GRAVEL PELTING CAR FENDERS as faculty, students and sports fans drive around the perimeter road at Galesburg High School is now in the past. Pleasantly paved streets, a foreign language and a refurbished lunchroom are all recent updates in my daily schedule at GHS.

Those pesky pebbles, clinging for life at the edge of the road, only to be flung into the grass by future NASCAR drivers are no longer. They were exchanged this summer for a smoother, sharper-looking blacktop drive, complete with anti-Indy 500 speed bumps. In turn, my fellow classmates no longer stress about careening their new Mustangs or Jeeps through deep, treacherous potholes leaving a cloud of gray dust to hang in the air.

As for the foreign language, may I say French class is going "tre bien" (very well)! My teacher, Monsieur Nusbaum, gave everyone the opportunity to choose their French name on the first day of class. Now I'm not sure if it's from reading all of those "Peanuts" comics or watching re-runs of old television shows, but the name "Lucie" caught my eye in a heartbeat. Although I could never be mistaken for an actual native of Paris, I have learned a couple general statements in French, such as "bonjour, ca va?" which is "hello, how are you?" and "au revoir" which is "see you later." Outside of class, I'll try to throw in a little bit of my newfound vocabulary here and there when I converse with my parents or chat online with friends.

In the middle of French, my classmates and I head downstairs toward the cafeteria for B lunch. Like the new asphalt outside, the cafeteria remodel was another project this summer at the high school. Last year, at one of my 7 a.m. student council meetings, a couple of people spoke about giving the lunch room a little bit of a "face lift." The former black zigzags on the lunchroom walls have been modernized to cool blues and light greens. New lounge furniture has been installed, providing another place for everyone to read their history books or snack on granola bars. Oh, and I must not forget to mention another big change, our new principal, Mr. Tom Chiles.

The new year at GHS feels like we're off to a great start with only a few intentional bumps in the road. Or shall I say, "tre magnifique"?

Answer the Door, It's Mr. Opportunity

SEPTEMBER 9

MR. OPPORTUNITY IS FOREVER KNOCKING AT THE HIGH SCHOOL DOORS.

One of the greatest perks about GHS is the vast opportunities it offers my classmates and me. For instance, if students want to "pump some iron" but don't have a YMCA pass, the weight room is always open until 4:30 Monday through Thursday to help put some muscle on the bones of a skinny teenager.

For the future editors and journalists of the world, the Budget gives students a feel for the pressure that comes with scrambling to meet a deadline, as well as what it's like to have others review your work. Students with dreams of being in the spotlight or those who get a rush out of public speaking class, can join the speech team or try out for the annual school play.

One opportunity almost all students can take advantage of involves just showing up to school. Starting Tuesday and running through Sept.

22, a select number of students from the class with the best attendance will be chosen to shave Mr. Tom Chiles's head at the homecoming assembly! Speaking of which, the calendar is marching toward the much-anticipated homecoming parade. Those students with skills in any type of art or carpentry are encouraged to help in that fun-loving adventure of building the class float.

For those of us who are always thinking outside the box, or even the country, GHS offers students the opportunity to travel to distant lands through AFS, the American Field Service. Closer to home, juniors and seniors can plan visits to the colleges of their dreams or visit the GHS Web site where they can find all kinds of college preparation information from counselors.

As for me, last week I was fortunate enough to grab the opportunity to attend the State Farm Classic Golf Tournament in Springfield with a couple of my golf teammates, thanks to coach Lorraine Gottenborg, who conveniently had extra tickets. We got to see the payoff for spending countless hours on the driving range and putting greens as the pros nailed shot after shot with ease.

Yes, Mr. Opportunity is alive and well at GHS. But it is wise to remember that even when opportunity does knock, a person still has to get off his seat and answer the door. And if for some reason, opportunity fails to knock, follow Milton Berle's advice: "Build a door!"

Golf Course No Place to Cut Loose

SEPTEMBER 16

LATELY, I HAVE BEEN SLICING MY DRIVES, BLADING MY CHIPS AND overshooting like a ball-hog on a basketball court. Ponds, flower gardens, restroom, corn fields - each time I hit a golf ball it seems to magnetize itself to everything on the course, but the pin.

When I set up to a shot, squirrels hide and trees duck. But if I were to become frustrated every time I made a bad shot, I'd never enjoy the game. Golf takes skill, patience, focus and, most of all, the ability to keep your chin up.

A prime example would be my drive on the third hole earlier this week at Lake Bracken. It was a rather cold and harsh Tuesday afternoon as I stood on the soggy tee box, studying the hole like a biologist examining an amoeba. To the right, a fortress of trees lurked from tee to green in a narrow cluster, while the left remained spotless except for a few isolated pine trees.

"OK, Jane, all you have to do is hit the ball left," I thought to myself. I bit my lip, raised my club high in the air and ... "Dink!" I stood in absolute horror and disbelief as I saw my Top Flite XL roll a measly three feet to my left.

At this point I could have a) scorned myself and lost all hope for the next round, b) chucked my driver into the nearby brush, or c) decided how to make the next drive better and maintain a positive outlook. I thought about answer "a" in my mind, but from past experiences chose to "keep my cool" and stick with option "c."

This is my second year on the GHS girls golf team and I've had to grin and bear it through many bad holes. What keeps me plugging away are those reassuring comments from my teammates, coach, and parents at the end of a disappointing round.

My personal goal this season is simple – to consistently keep the ball in the bland, short grass of the fairway and remind myself that Rome was not built in a day. I wonder how you say "fore!" in Italian?

Homecoming ala 1986 a Bit Gnarly

SEPTEMBER 23

- -

THIS MORNING WAS QUITE DIFFERENT FROM ANY OTHER. THE Go-Go's "We Got the Beat" blasted from my alarm clock at 5:31 a.m. I timidly dressed in black leggings, a neon T-shirt, off-the-shoulder sweat-shirt, huge hoop earrings, hair in a scrunchie to the side, and gobs of jewelry! Did I mention I was looking totally bodacious?

This week, GHS has gone back to a time of big hair, acid wash jeans, and Cindi Lauper songs like "Girls Just Wanna Have Fun." Examples of this year's homecoming theme, "That's So '80s," can be found hanging in the gnarly hallways, in our totally tubular classrooms and worn by our very own dudes and dudettes.

Tickets to this year's dance are miniature Rubik's Cubes that double as key chains for students who, like me, tend to lose such things. Another obvious sign of this year's homecoming theme can be seen in all the halls as my fellow classmates sport their electric blue or neon yellow "That's So '80s" T-shirts. Powder Puff teams also contributed with team mascots from the '80s era with names such as "Senior Smurfs" and "Junior Care Bears."

On Thursday, the entire student body was encouraged to dress as if we attended GHS 20 years back. Blue eye shadow, feathered bangs, and kids wearing their parents' 20-year-old clothes made the scene look straight out of "Saved by the Bell." I suddenly see why so many people cringe when they hear about our theme!

Students also had the chance to answer trivia questions to test their knowledge of the '80s each day this week. Even the faculty got involved in the theme by posting up unnamed pictures of themselves 20 years ago. My fellow classmates and I were challenged to match each photo with the correct teacher. And what a challenge it was for some!

This year's homecoming assembly also should be a blast from the past. A few teachers have volunteered to demonstrate the "Super Bowl Shuffle" that was performed by the Chicago Bears in 1985. A couple of students from each class will compete in a game involving the girls coming up with the best '80s costume for the guys. GHS Principal Mr. Chiles also will be announcing which class had the best attendance and therefore who will get to shave his head! That's wicked awesome!

Experiencing the '80s "lingo" and upbeat music has been a blast, but I'll be glad to get back to the 21st century on Monday. Besides, this Rubik's Cube is making me CRAZY!

If Superhero's Out, How about Editor?

SEPTEMBER 30

- -

WHAT DO I WANT TO BE WHEN I GROW UP?

This is an overwhelming yet fun question I have been asked since I was 5 years old ... and at the ripe old age of 15, I still don't have a clear answer. In kindergarten, I had my heart set on becoming a horse (yes, a horse) on my 35th birthday. I guess I watched "The Swan Princess" too many times.

However, as I soon grew to realize I would always be in human form, my future plans changed. At 8 years old, I was determined to become a veterinarian, until I was faced with the tragic death of my pet goldfish. I had a hard time flushing him away in the "toilet of termination."

Sometimes, I would be influenced to change my career path when I watched an inspiring movie or got lost in a page-turner. For instance, I remember tucking my older brother's tattered blankie under my shirt collar and jumping off the swing set with my arms wide open trying to "soar" in the air. Let's just say "Superman" has been too painful to watch ever since.

A new career-inspired opportunity at GHS for students who enjoy helping others learn is called "Tomorrow's Teachers." I know without attending a single meeting that I could never be a teacher. With low scores in the patience department, I would find it difficult to sit down with a group of students and teach them their ABCs or 123s. But I have great admiration for those who can simultaneously instruct 27 different person-alities and learning styles in repetitious skills like punctuation marks or long division with fractions.

Currently, I am looking at a career as a fashion magazine editor. I have been writing short stories and narratives since I was about 7 years old, and I love it. As for fashion, I recently got into watching shows like "Project Runway" and look forward to televised red-carpet events such as the Oscars, just to watch the "Fashion Police" at work. Expressing myself is what I do best; writing and fashion are two great ways to bring out my voice, since I can't sing to save my life.

Who knows, maybe in 10 years, I'll be writing a feature story on the latest fashion comeback ... the cape!

Sibling Rivalry Fades with Growing Confidence

OCTOBER 7

- -

SIBLING RIVALRY IS A CHALLENGE MOST BROTHERS AND SISTERS FACE no matter how old they are. At age 3, my older brother, John, already had me labeled as a Class A pest. Every Saturday morning, John would systematically organize his Hot Wheels according to size, color and speed. Then, here I came dressed in pink polka dot pajamas and pigtails like a wild goose let loose. I loved to see how mad he got. Now, after 10 years of following my brother through Silas, Churchill and GHS, I can say without hesitation that there are some definite pros and cons to being the baby in the family.

Having a big brother who was quite involved in school, I was always stuck spending my evenings at either a windy baseball game or a crowded band concert. But as the years passed, I began to realize some positives in my brother. When my parents refused to no longer play the role of "Driving Miss Jane," it was John and his Monte Carlo who stepped up to take me to the big basketball game or to Pizza Hut to meet my friends.

Regrettably, there will always be at least one teacher who mentions what a good student my brother was or how fun he was to have in class. I love my brother, but I know exactly how Jan Brady felt in the "Brady Bunch" as she complains that it's all about "Marsha, Marsha, Marsha!" I cannot run fast enough to escape being in the shadow of my brother. Geesh, even my name is a female spin-off of John!

It seems that I am always trying to compete with this person. Whether it be a simple game of Go Fish or quarterly grade point averages, I can't help but feel a certain instinctive drive to surpass him. I suppose this is the same for my classmates as well, especially during the high school years. I have slowly come to realize there are some skills my brother has that I'll never catch up with, such as figuring out those impossible calculus equations or simply juggling a soccer ball. I have become content with this, finally understanding that I have my own strengths and do not have to step in the same footprints in the road set by the almighty John.

Now that he is off at college, there are no Hot Wheels to scatter and I will soon be chauffeuring myself down West Fremont Street with the pain of sibling rivalry wearing off. Unbelievably, I'm looking forward to my big brother's next return home.

"Got any sevens?"

"Go fish, John."

No Rrretreat, No Surrender

OCTOBER 14

- -

LEARNING FRENCH IS LIKE TRYING TO WRITE WITH YOUR OPPOSITE hand. At first, the language is just like they describe it in the course catalog - foreign. But after days and weeks of practicing the same routine, it eventually becomes more natural.

After watching Disney's "The Hunchback of Notre Dame" at 7 years old, I knew France was the country for me. Not only is Paris known for the grand Eiffel Tower, it is also famous for being the "Fashion Capitol" of the world.

When I was younger, I grew up watching Madeline, a cartoon about a young girl who lived in an orphanage in Paris. One of my favorite aspects of the show was the way the young girls talked, especially how they would rhythmically roll the sounds of specific consonants from their mouths. For about a month, I tried to fit into conversation as many words as I could that started with the letter R. I think my parents got rrreally, rrreally wrrrung out with this rrroutine.

Eight years later, I am enrolled in French I with Mr. Nusbaum and am finding there is a lot more to learning the language than rolling a few R's. Some of the difficulties include knowing where to put the accents and pronouncing the words correctly. While this is challenging, trying to remember what each of these strange sounding words mean is often quite confusing.

Every so often, vocabulary comes easy when words such as "intelligent" or "patient" are the same as in English. Oral exams are especially tough because the speaker on the tape tends to talk extremely fast, making it hard to respond. In addition, I seem to constantly forget that my name is "Lucie," not Jane.

We have done several French-based projects. Everyone wrote a report on a European country and presented it in class. We described our favorite celebrity in the foreign tongue and have drawn mock campaign signs. We used lots of fun activities to help us remember the basics, such as bingo and drawing connect the dot pictures with the help of a French speaking partner. A class favorite is a DVD trivia game with half of the room competing with the other, all answers in French, of course.

I'm also in French Club and hoping it will be a fun time. I'm sure it will be, though I once heard someone from another school say he was in the French Club and they didn't do anything. They just sat around and, every once in a while, surrendered to the German Club!

Marching, Playing and All That Jazz

OCTOBER 21

- -

"MAN, IF YOU GOTTA ASK YOU'LL NEVER KNOW!" - A QUOTE BY ONE OF the greatest jazz legends of all time, Louis Armstrong, is also the theme for this year's GHS Marching Streaks field show. With get up and dance songs like "Sing, Sing, Sing" and "God Bless the Child" this season has been truly ... jazzy!

Already, the last week of marching band is under way and today we will be entering our final competition of the season at the University of

Illinois Festival of Bands. The U of I competition is on par with going to state in sports. The week before is nothing but practice, practice, practice. With after-school rehearsals Tuesday and Thursday and one dress rehearsal Friday, my fellow band mates and I have been critiqued on everything from keeping our toes up to pointing our chins at the sky.

In order to help us really get the feeling and emotions of any song we play, our directors often provide us with the story behind the musical selection. Take the song "God Bless the Child" about famous jazz singer Billie Holiday and her trials and triumphs in life. Once I knew the real story of that composition, I no longer needed to see the dynamics written on paper, because I could feel them as I sympathized with the song in my heart.

Although the actual marching is enjoyable and exciting, my favorite part of the U of I competition is the enchanting experience of watching the Marching Illini work their way smoothly across Memorial Stadium. It's quite interesting to see the many forms and cool moves that a larger, more experienced college band can create. The Marching Illini are also a great role model for many of my bandmates as some of them are hoping to pursue future careers in music.

It seems like just yesterday I was learning new moves to "Sing, Sing, Sing" in hot, sticky August weather, impatiently waiting for the cool fall temperatures to arrive. Now that it is mid-October, it is now time to shine my mellophone bell, brighten up my marching kicks, and keep my shoulders to the front on those tricky slide steps (I hear U of I has some rough Astroturf).

In the words of another smooth jazz player, Jane Simkins, "If you're gonna trip you might as well look good doing it!"

Plain Jane Transforms Herself on Halloween

OCTOBER 28

- -

WHY DIDN'T THE SKELETON GO TRICK-OR-TREATING? HE HAD NO BODY to go with!

Oh, how I love Halloween. Leaves once lost in a sea of green now lay underfoot as unique individuals in layered shades of orange and red on the sidewalks of my Prairie Street neighborhood. Gap-toothed jack-o'-lanterns smile from almost every front porch as friends and I scurry from house to house in search of our favorite treats.

Be certain to stop at the Kanes' and Knuths' while making sure to leave room in the bag for the really huge candy bar at the Adcocks'. Hurry home for the hot apple cider and the annual trading of the treats. I always tried to barter my hard and sour candy for anything containing either chocolate or peanut butter.

The costume is probably my favorite thing about Halloween. It's the one chance for an out-of-body experience, dressing up as someone or "something" other than plain old Jane for the night. I remember the fun I had as the Flamenco dancer in Mr. Rux's fifth grade class at Silas. Wearing a colorful skirt and a bright red flower in my hair as if I stepped right out of a Spanish textbook. When I asked my friend Alexa about one of her top costumes, she told about dressing as a businessman last year, suitcase and all.

At 15, I'm a little old for door-to-door trick-or-treating, but I still have many opportunities to enjoy my favorite holiday. The best way to get into the feel of the season and bump my heart rate up a few notches is by taking in a classic scary movie with Freddie Krueger or Jason on the AMC channel. But the most fun might be on West Fremont Street, where an advantage of being in the GHS Student Council is coming up with your own costume for Haunted High School. This year, my friend Emily and I have decided to dress up as cowgirls while we pass out Jolly Ranchers and Cow Tails to the elementary students. Some of my fellow members are very creative when it comes to dressing up for Halloween. My friend Matt has chosen to be the infamous Pillsbury Doughboy. With a three-foot whisk and a big floppy chef's hat, everyone will be trying to tickle him just to hear the famous Doughboy giggle.

Halloween is full of creepy candy, freaky movies and ghoulish costumes, but what are the scariest seven digits on November 1? The phone number to your family dentist!

Wienerschnitzel Among Food Day Adventures

NOVEMBER 4

WHAT'S THAT FAMILIAR, YET INDISTINCT SMELL COMING FROM THE language hallway? Burritos? Spinach bisque? Perhaps fettucini alfredo? Or could it be.....yes, I think it is.....Wienerschnitzel?

Strangely enough, I think it's all of them. As a foreign language novice, Thursday was my first time experiencing International Food Day and I'm still recovering from those extra spicy, Spanish tacos.

Food Day is all about students gaining new culinary experiences and one of mine was cooking with instructions more in depth than: "open can" and "boil in pan". The French are famous for their fantastic bakeries, especially ones that sell those mouth-watering pastries. So, as I Googled my way through an online cookbook in search of my contribution to Food Day, I came across a "Crème Puffs" recipe and was immediately drawn to the simplicity of the ingredients: water, eggs, salt, and flour. As for the filling, the only requirement was to spray aerosol whipped cream into the inside of the pastry. Surely, anyone can fill a jelly doughnut? However, the simplicity of the recipe stopped after the ingredients. Believe it or not, the toughest part of the process was spraying in the filling. As I pumped in the whipped cream, it began to melt and then soak into the pastry, leaving only a small amount of filling.

Unfortunately, I did not realize this until a classmate presented me with one of my 13 soggy, barren puffs. It turns out there was a special crème recipe made just for the filling of the pastry, and no, "remove tab and spray" was not one of the instructions.

Another of my Food Day adventures was sampling new dishes from other cultures, some of which I'd never heard. In the Spanish section, my amigo Maria's Mexican cheesecake was at the top of my list. A mixture of cinnamon, chocolate, cheesecake, and other deliciously rich ingredients, one bite of that and I was already digging for my Alka-Seltzer.

One Latin cuisine caught me a little off guard. It as so spicy I almost called 911 to extinguish the flames burning in my mouth. I sampled some of the German dishes, but those 15-letter words are just too hard to pronounce. Ever try to spell-check Wienerschnitzel?

Food Day gave me a new appreciation for international cuisine, but it also reminded me how fortunate I am for simple delicacies like apple pie and Cracker Jacks.

Planning the Future Easy With a Few Tests

NOVEMBER 11

- -

IT ALL STARTED WITH A SLIP OF PAPER. ...

About a month ago, a notice for an upcoming test was laid upon my desk. However, the only part of the letter that caught my attention was the word "test." The PLAN Test does precisely what its name says; it prepares college-bound students for the future ACT and SAT exams. Figuring a little test prep couldn't hurt, I strolled down to the book room and signed myself up.

About two weeks later, I entered the wonderful world of multiple choice as I walked into a room with a sign that read "PLAN Test 7:30 a.m. to 11 a.m." I chose a seat near the back between two of my good friends, Emma and Caitlin. Two freshly sharpened No. 2 pencils, one scientific calculator, and one handy-dandy pink eraser were all I brought with me, not to mention my thinking cap.

Once the first hour bell rang and we recited the Pledge of Allegiance, the counselors passed out the test booklets and answer sheets. But before we dove into the questions, we had to fill out a survey on our interests and future career ideas. Then came the tough part. One hundred fifty minutes of racking my brain and trying to stay inside the lines as I shaded in my answers,

Fast forward to Tuesday of this past week, or as I like to call it, Judgment Day. During chemistry, I received a bright orange pass from my counselor to collect my PLAN Test results. Walking to the counselors' office, my heart was beating like a drummer in a rock band.

What if I filled in my answers on the wrong side? What if my scores were so bad that the grading machine busted a fuse from checking all my incorrect responses? What if all this college stuff was just too hard?

Fortunately, my outrageous fears were put to rest when Mrs. Riggins presented my results and explained to me the meaning of each score. The most fun part of looking over my results was in the career placement area. Based on my scores in reading, math, English and science, the computer matched me with a list of potential careers that line up with my talents. Discovering that I had some aptitude in the fields of social science and medical diagnosis was a little surprising, but the creative and applied arts side of me seemed to fit like a glove.

In the last two years, I have learned that high school is great for providing tests that let you know what life may be like when you're old, like 25 or 30. Last year, I found some useful results in the area of male companionship and now I know what my future career may entail.

I wonder what slip of paper will be the next to land on my desk. My driver's permit? I think any credible test would match me up nicely with a BMW!

When Viral Defenses Fail, Laughter Best Medicine

NOVEMBER 18

- -

TIME TO PUT THE DOCTOR'S NUMBER ON SPEED DIAL, BREAK OUT THE antibacterial soap and stock up on boxes of Kleenex. The flu has struck the home of the Streaks.

I'm sure the nurse's office has recently looked a lot like Macy's the day after Thanksgiving: full of customers. Two of my teachers were out sick Wednesday and the names of a countless number of my classmates were missing on the attendance sheet.

There are basically two main types of the flu: respiratory and stomach. Thankfully, my immune system has not yet been attacked by either, (knock on wood), and I've been pondering how to keep it that way.

Perhaps I should employ the "Boxer Strategy." Stay clear of a red nose or any potential knockout punches by bobbing and weaving through the hallways and keeping out of the clinches of infected opponents. Some other tactical considerations might be:

Viral Defense Tactic #1.) "The Girl in the Plastic Bubble." If John Travolta can do it why can't I?

Viral Defense Tactic #2.) "Face Mask." I walk around school with a gas mask that filters any harmful germs that may enter my lungs. Of course, French will be twice as hard trying to pronounce vocabulary in muffled "Darth-Vaderish" tones.

Viral Defense Tactic #3.) "Back Away Spray." I keep a can of Lysol strapped to my side. If my lab partner's looking a tad pale (here's where the Lysol comes into play), I'll ask if she would like to borrow some "perfume" and cover her in disinfectant. With sinuses stuffed like a Thanksgiving turkey, she'll never know!

Although I have little doubt these ideas could work, I think I'll just stick to the good ol'-fashioned way to stay healthy: get plenty of rest and wash my hands as often as possible.

And if, somehow, my plan to stay germ-free does not work out and that achy-breaky chill starts up my spine, I know exactly what my "Feel-better Soon" kit would include: "I Love Lucy" movies, warm chicken broth loaded with oyster crackers, Seven -Up, my favorite cozy quilt, and the comics section of The Register-Mail (laughter is the best medicine).

Much to Be Thankful For at GHS

NOVEMBER 25

- -

With Thanksgiving this week, here is my list of why I am thankful for being a student at Galesburg High School.

1.) Athletics. Whether it's swinging a bat or shooting a ball, the Silver Streaks are a force to be reckoned with. Being a student at GHS, I have a plethora of options when it comes to playing sports. If I crave the thrill of diving for a ball flying 90 miles an hour at the floor, the volleyball team is an excellent choice. However, if I'm not the "contact sport" type of athlete, there's always Galesburg's top-notch swim team. Oh yeah, and did I mention this year's Boys cross country team received the "Home Town Hero" award?

2.) Music Program. This year's 2006 Marching Streaks brought some serious hardware home when we received grand champion at our first competition and took third place at the U of I competition. The buck doesn't stop there. Jazz band, pep band and concert band are filled with my fellow classmates who are young, yet extremely talented musicians. And if you can't toot a horn or beat a drum, singing in the one of the many choral groups may be for you. This fantastic music program helps make GHS the well-rounded, diverse school it is.

3.) Clubs. Each club at GHS has a specific purpose that often ends up benefiting the school, community and students themselves. Take Key Club for instance. Its main goal is to make a difference through numerous volunteer projects in the community. Members have been known to rake leaves for the elderly, organize can food drives and help serve at the annual Kiwanis Pancake Day.

4.) School Spirit. Whoever said California held all the gold had obviously never visited a Galesburg High School basketball game. All someone would have to do to realize how much GHS supports its athletes is to attend an event at John Thiel Gym and take a glance at the student section. Trying to scope someone out in that colossal mass of yellow Streaks T-shirts is like hunting for "Waldo."

5.) Choices. Garden salad or cheese pizza? Dance II or Individual Fitness? Bass clarinet or sousaphone? So many choices and only four years. Making a variety of daily decisions, good or bad, forces me to create my own destiny.

At times, school may feel a little monotonous, as if I'm on autopilot. But for the most part, I am greatly thankful for life on Fremont Street as it is reflected on my plate, or should I say palate, as I sit down for Thanksgiving dinner. The basics of the bird, potatoes, dressing and rolls are flavored and colored with the singular tastes of cranberries, green beans and Grandma's five-cup salad. After all, like high school, you are what you eat. Or as the great poet "Popeye" would say, "I yam what I yam and that's all that I yam."

Bells and Whistles Great Way to Show Spirit

DECEMBER 2

- -

WE PUMP UP THE CROWD AND THE TEAM, WE REPRESENT GOOD OL' GHS in uniform, and we perform during halftime at home basketball games. Who are we? Here's a hint, we're neither spunky cheerleaders nor groovy Gadets. We are the Galesburg High School pep band.

With only four or five home football games each year, boys and girls basketball season provides us with numerous opportunities to strut our stuff. Therefore, there are two pep bands at GHS, the "Silver" and the "Gold." Some kids enjoy playing "Hi-Ho Silver" so much, they express their passion for music at both "Silver" and "Gold" performances!

Whenever I hear the word "basketball" one song in particular comes to mind. "Hey Baby" is like the national anthem of all pep band songs.

I'll forever be able to recall that catchy chorus being sung by both fans and athletes in John Thiel Gymnasium. Popular tunes such as "Rocky" and "Twist and Shout" also top my pep band "Billboard Chart." Then, of course, there's the traditional ditty every Silver Streak hears while attending a football or basketball game, "William Tell."

GHS was nearly arrested by the fashion police at last year's girls game versus arch-rival Alleman when half of our Silver Streaks bleachers were covered in green. Galesburg fans were confused as to why our own pep band was dressed in the opposing team's school colors. The explanation for the wardrobe malfunction was that the forest green harmonized perfectly with our marching band theme, "Medieval Knights." Thankfully, we won't be receiving any style citations this year. Our shirts are "Silver Streaks Silver" with a hint of "Galesburg Gold," just enough to make it obvious which team we're supporting.

Every now and then, a GHS band alum will dust off his or her instrument and join in with our pep band for old time's sake. It may take awhile for them to remember the lively rhythm of "Louie, Louie" but eventually, the familiar tune sparks their memory and soon they're back in high school.

We may not have flashy pompoms or fancy dance routines, but with our own instruments of pep, we share our recipe for team spirit: oodles of brass, woodwinds and percussion, with an occasional dash of cow bell.

Could Super Snowman be Her Next Record?

DECEMBER 9

- -

JANUARY 28, 2000: JANE BREAKS HER OWN POGO-STICK RECORD BY hopping around the living room for 15 minutes straight. Thankfully, no animals or valuables were harmed in the process.

Breaking a record is like trying to create the perfect chocolate chip cookie. You must have profuse determination, strong work habits, and perseverance to achieve such a goal. While browsing through the athletics page of the Galesburg High School Web site, I discovered a series of all-time records in each sport. Records in some track and field events were especially astonishing. For instance, in 1999, Pierre Woods set the school high jump record as he lifted himself 6 feet 8 inches into the air, or as I think of it, about one and a half feet over my head! This golf season, I was fortunate enough to witness our captain, Amanda Mendrek, make Silver Streaks history as she established a new girls' record shooting a 33 (nine holes) at our Aledo meet. One of our teachers, Ms. Kniker (alias Ms. Myers), made her mark at GHS about 15 years ago when she took first place honors at the Western Big Six cross country meet. I was also able to observe a record-breaking soccer game my freshman year when Kiara Akpore matched the record set by Nicole Welch (2001) with four goals scored in one game!

Athletics isn't the only place where GHS students have been remembered for a great achievement. I could probably name off a few of my buddies who hold special records of their own. Let's see, how many cartons of milk drunk in one lunch period? Most tardies ever received in one term? Fastest time traveled from the west to the east wing of GHS? The number of textbooks carried at one time? Or, how about, most money charged on a lunch card in one swipe?

Yeesh, thinking of all these high achievements sure is inspiring. I wonder what sort of record I could break? I'm pretty good when it comes to staring contests. Maybe I could set the record for the longest amount of time spent without blinking. There's also my other hidden talent, shopping. Guess I'll have to chat with my parents about that one. (Glances outside.) Wait a minute, that's an impressive mass of snow out there, which gives me an idea. I'll need a carrot, two sticks, 3 buttons, and a scarf. ... World's Tallest Snowman, here I come!

GHS Band Breaks into Wrap Scene

DECEMBER 16

SCENTED CANDLES, COOKIE DOUGH, CANDY BARS, ICE CREAM SOCIAL tickets, oh my!

This holiday season, the Galesburg High School Band Boosters are putting the "fun" back into fundraising. Most often, school money-making ventures are targeted at the weakness of their customers ... the taste buds. I could probably build a new wing on GHS with all the mini pizzas, fruit baskets, and cheesecakes my brother and I have sold (and consumed) over the years. So, it was nice to be able to break the "sweet tooth" strategy and take a different approach to collecting donations from the community. No longer must I wear out every doorbell and reliable customer in the 900 block of Prairie Street, while bearing the wrath of the petite, yet ferocious, Schnauzer across the street. Instead, I can help out the Marching Streaks while simultaneously sitting in the center of Sandburg Mall. It almost seems too good to be true!

Stationed directly across from the Fashion Bug and Hibbett Sports and with the assistance and blessing of our parents, my fellow bandmates and I are making wrap music. That's right. Not "rap" like most parents skip by when scanning the radio channels, but the kind that goes around Christmas presents. We are heavily into wrapping ... any present, any size, for anyone ... free (donations welcome)! I must admit I tend to shy away from the actual wrapping aspect, (folding, as in laundry, and I just don't get along). I prefer designing fancy bows and ribbons to adorn the beautiful packages. One funny observation was that most of our customers were of the male gender. They must have trouble with the creases, too.

Though this particular fundraiser has provided me with more than a couple of paper cuts the past two Decembers, it also has given me a sense of the generosity and kindness that exist in our community. Some shoppers have gone so far as to offer donations without asking for a single one of their gifts to be wrapped. Whether its pocket change, five dollars, or a simple "thank you," every ounce of gratuity goes to make our band program what it is today - fantastic!

As I checked my calendar this morning, I noticed I'm scheduled to work again this Saturday. I think it's time for me to take the chance, break out of my comfort zone, and attempt to lay a little wrap music of my own on an unassuming customer's package. Buyers beware!

GHS Stuco Delivers Holiday Spirit

DECEMBER 23

- -

"HOME - YOU COVER THE GARLAND. PRIDE - TACKLE THE WRAPPING paper. School Relations - I want those wreaths hanging on the walls in a jolly fashion A.S.A.P! The Christmas Tree needs to be ship-shape, and remember, we never leave an ornament behind!" Project Holiday is under way!

As the Yuletide season gathers steam, Student Council's Project Holiday is churning toward Christmas with a full head of cheer both inside and outside the halls of Galesburg High School. As StuCo members deck the school walls from ceiling to floor in red and green, others are busy as elves collecting toys for the less fortunate, good girls and boys of our community. Others are busy attending one of my favorite events of Project Holiday, the annual caroling trip to local nursing homes. Our short time with the residents of The Marigold and Seminary Manor is a gift that leaves each of us wondering if we are the giver or the receiver.

As any unfortunate person within earshot of me in church knows, singing has never been one of my strong suits, so my friends were not exactly following me in merry measure. Despite this obvious fact, you won't catch me backing down from belting out a chorus of "White Christmas" or refraining from a refrain of "Silent Night." And though our unpolished group of teenagers did not have the dreamy sound of "Choral Dynamics," we still got quite a few smiles along the way. As we paraded down each hallway there was always at least one resident singing along with us as we passed their rooms. Some even made requests! With a booklet of about 15 traditional holiday tunes, I'm sure we crooned "Frosty the Snowman" at least six times. In order to make the entertainment even sweeter, we handed out festive, mini-candy canes along our musical trek. If we could not please the ears, at least we could stimulate the taste buds.

As we left each nursing home, I remembered how good it was to do something out of the norm that brightened someone's day. Realizing that I was in no danger of melting like Frosty on this unseasonably mild December day, I couldn't help but echo his final sentiments. "Goodbye, don't you cry, we'll be back again someday."

What Will the New Year Bring?

DECEMBER 30

AS I WAVE GOODBYE TO 2006, I LOOK FORWARD TO WHAT THE BIG '07 has in store for me. That wonderful, little piece of plastic that allows me to chauffeur myself to soccer practice? Or possibly, I'll finally beat my dad in a round of Trivial Pursuit by capitalizing on my newly found knowledge from history class? Or perhaps, those two summers spent sweating in the Voyles Field concession stand will help me land a Seminary Street job waiting on someone with more than Super Nachos in mind.

Make sure to look both ways when walking down the sidewalk this year. Jane Simkins will be hitting the road for her first time. Yes, I can finally put away the plastic Little Tike steering wheel (ages 3 and up) and really put the pedal to the metal after driver's ed this summer. Of course, getting those 50 hours of adult-supervised drive time won't be easy. But I'm sure my parents won't mind riding in the family truckster with me manning the gears! Let's see, the brake is which one?

It's also time for me to dust off the old TI-34 Calculator and brush up on my memorization skills. Final exams are the 12th of January, which means a brand-new spring schedule of classes will soon be coming my way. I wonder what new terms I'll be adding to my foreign language vocabulary in French 2. Gone are the blissful days of reading classic literature in Mrs. Qualls' class, as well as the exciting experiments in chemistry. As the sun makes a little longer arc in the sky each day, the moment to kick my brain into high gear for geometry has arrived. The school year has reached the turnaround point and I can almost see the finish line of my sophomore year in the distance!

Not only will "Sixteen Candles" be my 2007 theme song, but I will also be officially joining the ranks of the "Upper Class" at GHS, something that comes with a lot of perks. One benefit that I am especially anticipating is making college visits, a great opportunity to check out what different schools have to offer and tour their campuses. I've already got a few schools in the back of my mind. I hope New York University isn't too long of a drive. Maybe I can get my 50 hours of driving time in!

It's promising to know I can look forward to 2007 with excitement and a positive outlook. But first things first. Better get my feet back on the ground, my head into the textbooks, and finish before I start again. Are finals ever really final?

The Ultimate Inspiration is the Deadline

JANUARY 6

- -

I STARE AT THE BLANK PIECE OF PAPER IN FRONT OF ME AS AN ARTIST does a vacant canvas. The pen is as mighty as the sword, I remind myself. Boy, writing sure can be intimidating, especially when it's an unadorned notebook or a blank computer monitor just waiting for an attention-grabber to begin its life story.

Like any medicine, journalism comes with side effects, both physical and emotional. I'm talking hand cramps, eye problems, headaches and in some cases, extreme irritability. However, the other 99.9% of the time, writing brings great satisfaction and, often, hours of laughter.

Recently in English class, we tackled our third and final writing assessment, or as I like to call it, 40 minutes of seclusion. I'm not exactly sure, but I think these assessments are given to provide feedback to teachers and other educators on the relative writing skills of middle school and high school students in the district. At the high school level, we usually are provided a time limit of around 40 to 45 minutes to complete the essay from the given prompt.

The moment my English teacher, Mrs. Qualls, gave my classmates and me the go-ahead, the "chitter-chatter" of voices in Room 45 was turned from maximum volume to mute in one breath. I could hear Ticonderoga pencils scrabbling across thin sheets of paper all around me. My fellow classmates and I were each zoned in on our own thoughts, ideas and opinions, with nothing else in mind.

Mrs. Qualls announced when we had 20, then 10 minutes left before the bell was to ring. With about seven minutes left, every test-taker's worst fear draped upon me, the Big Blankout. I sat at my desk, eyeing the stark space at the bottom of my third page, waiting for a brilliant conclusion to enter my thoughts.

"Five minutes!" Mrs. Qualls announced. Out of the corner of my eye I saw students stapling their papers and handing them in with a sign of relief on their faces.

"Two minutes!" Focus, Jane, focus on the task at hand, I told myself. Just when all hope was almost lost, I pulled a "Little Engine that Could," and whipped out a quick and to-the-point grand finale.

Writing provides a healthy way for me to express my ideas, journal the ups and downs of life, and lets my voice be heard. Hey, what happened to that blank piece of paper?

Mary Poppins, Where are You?

JANUARY 13

- -

WRINKLED T-SHIRTS, MISMATCHED SOCKS, DINGY RUNNING SHOES - and is that Monday night's Tuna Helper?

As of now, my room is a complete and utter disaster. Anyone walking into it would think my closet exploded or my room was struck by a tornado. From the messy aftermath, the cause is quite obvious: 'twas the infamous and dreaded "Finals Week."

If I had to rank my chores, cleaning my room would take last place. Dusting the window sills, shelves and fan feels like Allergy Kingdom. My eyes water, my nose gets stuffed, and dust seems to linger in the air for hours. Folding and hanging up mountain-high stacks of clothes is always a drag. Don't even get me started on making my bed!

Yes, without a little creativity, or at least some cool tunes, cleaning my room can be a real bore. However, by adding a fun twist to my every-day chores, I can soon transform those 60 minutes of anguish into an hour of power!

Growing up with an older sibling, I loved to challenge my brother to any sort of race. Cleaning our rooms was one of them. Starting from our doorways, we would see who could make his or her bed or organize the bookshelves the quickest. Whoever won got his or her choice of the other's baseball cards. To make things more interesting, we would raise the stakes to cleaning the toilets or taking out the trash.

Music can make anything more enjoyable. Flip the switch on my radio and jam to the hottest hits while vacuuming the floor. This way, I can drown out the Dirt Devil and listen to the latest Beyonce tune.

If all else fails, a positive attitude is always the best medicine for the "Cleaning my Room Flu." Trying to keep my spirits up while hunting for the final dust-covered pieces of the holiday puzzle sprawled across my floor since Thanksgiving, can be a chore all by itself.

I'm not Mary Poppins, who returns everything back to order with a snap of a finger. I can sure tell you, though, we did not have Tuna Helper last Monday!

Without Friends, She'd be in Stressville

JANUARY 20

- -

FRIENDS ARE LIKE RULERS THAT STRAIGHTEN OUT MY PROBLEMS AND keep me from getting out of line. They also help me measure things, like when I get too self-absorbed or full of myself. With a kind zinger or two, they can quickly reel me back to reality.

Ever since that first day of kindergarten, I knew having friends would be crucial to surviving school. They held my place in the lunch line, convinced me my polka dot turtleneck and striped leggings looked great and taught me how to hang upside down on the monkey bars.

Sometimes, they helped me through the tough stuff. Like when I got picked last in dodge ball and one of my best buds, sensing my embarrassment, invited me to play hopscotch instead.

Nowadays, issues such as taking enough challenging classes with the hopes of being accepted to a prestigious university are always in the back of my mind. However, thanks to my friends pulling me out of "Stressville" every now and then, I'm enjoying most every day spent within the walls of GHS.

One of my favorite aspects of our high school is the diversity of students and how well our various personalities complement each other. I love being among my friends who are musicians and those who are athletes, all surrounding a lunch table and enjoying each other's company. I always look forward to hearing the outcome of last weekend's big basketball tournament from my pal Jenna while Matt, another comrade, enjoys bantering with me about our favorite styles of music.

My friends also provide me with a sense of comfort. Tuesday, I arrived in my new geometry class quickly scanning the student body in search of a familiar face. I was ecstatic to see my good ol' chum Lindsay stroll into the room. Tackling proofs and polygons should be no problem on the soccer bus this spring. A friend in need is a friend indeed!

Art Buchwald, Pulitzer Prize-winning satirist and beloved columnist passed away Wednesday at 81, living nearly a year longer than the prediction of his doctors. A well-known Buckwald quotation sums up my feelings about friendship: "The best things in life aren't things." You said it, Art.

She's Happy to Support Swim Team Like a Rock

JANUARY 27

- -

THE NIGHT WAS HUMID. THE SMELL OF CHLORINE PERMEATED THE building along with the cheers from fans and members of the GHS boys swim team. I am finally attending my first swim meet at GHS, a truly awesome experience that I will repeat next year.

The last time I was on a swim team, my arms were strapped to massive yellow floating devices and a pair of tie-dyed goggles were cutting off the circulation to my face. I was a walking, talking beach ball.

My first and only swim meet took place at Lake Bracken Country Club on the Fourth of July. I was the ripe old age of 4. The glare from the blistering July sun striking the blue water will always be fresh in my memory. My fellow participants and I had a parent guide us down the lanes and back just in case one of us decided to go "belly up." Sadly, I suffered from a severe case of the "sink like a rock" syndrome and my career as a swimmer never got off the bottom of the pool. After 11 years of never witnessing an actual swim meet, I broke my own record last Tuesday by paying a visit to my pals on the GHS boys swim team.

Though the ever-present smell of chlorine had led me to believe that, in fact, there was a pool in Wicall Gym, I had never actually seen it. As my good friend Emily led me toward the bleachers at Mustain Pool, I noticed swim meets had changed dramatically since preschool.

First off, in several races, the swimmers started the race by jumping from mini diving boards above the edge of the water. The swim meet "referee" announces, "Take your mark" and, once everyone was set, a single "beep" would sound allowing the race to begin. What I found most interesting were the various styles of swimming, none of which resembled my own unique version of the dog-paddle. I always thought a "fly" was just an annoying bug to be swatted. Strength and endurance are valuable ingredients to becoming a successful GHS swimmer, but the team camaraderie was equally impressive Tuesday night. I could do nothing but smile as I observed several of my classmates standing at the end of a teammate's lane encouraging him to stay strong as he raced on.

That night, the Streaks ended up winning the meet against Peoria Woodruff, due in large part to their success in the relays, proving that competitions are never won alone. I was happy to do my small part, cheering from the bleachers with Emily. After all, there's not much of a fashion statement that can be made with a swim cap, especially when accessorized with yellow floaties.

Ads on the Go: Say It with a Shirt

FEBRUARY 3

- -

SUPER BOWL SUNDAY IS THE FASHION SHOW OF ADVERTISING. Companies from across the spectrum flaunt their new commercials during timeouts of the biggest game of the year. Millions are spent on slick gimmicks ranging from your basic dancing monkeys to computer-generated Clydesdales.

Not to be outdone, Galesburg High School has fired up the marketing engine as well, even though the pigskin stopped flying around Van Dyke Field in October.

"T-shirts! Get your French Club, bowling, student council, marching band, (you name the activity, we've got it) T-shirts!" Rather than paying for a stationary billboard to attract new members or supporters of school organizations, most of the advertising and recruiting at GHS has become mobilized on the legs of a fashionable student body. In two years of high school, I've seen a silver streak on everything from flip-flops to duffel bags to golf tees! And though the Streaks logo comes in handy in the fairway when I have forgotten to label my golf ball, I can do without the all-too-frequent experience of having that same logo stare up at me through six inches of pond water.

I have also noticed that certain colors are very popular, and often, they aren't the revered silver, gold or black. Brighter, more standout colors such as raging red, hotter-than-hot pink and glow-in-the-dark lime green seem to be in high demand. In addition, a brash quip or inspirational quote usually accompanies this form of textile broadcasting. For instance, the Girls' golf team shirts read, "We may play the forward tees, but we don't take a back seat to anyone." Right on cue Thursday, the Girls basketball team locks up the Big 6 Championship at Quincy. I couldn't wait to see what clever phrase Courtney Knuth might have on her shirt Friday.

Posters are also highly recommended and productive ways of getting the word out. Swirl week starts this Monday and the hallways look as if the copy machine went crazy. Posters for events such as Battle of the Bands, Spirit Week, court elections and dance ticket sales cover the walls like a cotton sweater straight from the dryer. Intercom announcements in advisory always provide up to date information about upcoming practices and meetings along with the "Special of the Day" for lunch.

Whether you're a Bears fan or a Colts fan, surviving the exhausting hype of the pre-game and making it to kickoff is a great accomplishment. And whether its Rex or Peyton slapping on that championship hat just microseconds after the final whistle, glory, like advertising, is only momentary, fading quickly like cotton gone through too many washings. I have a drawer full of billboards to prove it.

Swirl Puts the Shoe On the Other Foot

FEBRUARY 10

- -

TAKE ONE, LIGHTS, CAMERA, AAAAND . . .. ACTION!

"Will you go to Swirl with me?" "Cut!" Take 2, "So, going to Swirl with anyone?" "Cut!" Take 3, "Hey, dude, feeling swirly?" The much-rehearsed line that makes any girl at GHS sweat. This year's Swirl theme is "A Red Carpet Affair." However, finding the date is an affair in itself!

"Roses are red, violets are blue" just doesn't cut it anymore when inviting someone to a high school dance. For a few of my more creative friends, asking a boy to Swirl has become more of an adventure in ingenuity. Take for instance, my friend Katie. She popped the question by spelling out "Swirl?" using french fries from the cafeteria during lunch.

Personally, I prefer to ask a boy "face-to-face" for that full instantaneous reaction. With various modes of communication these days, so many more options are opening up that are both quick and painless. A couple of my buddies opt for my second favorite way of inviting someone to a dance, the telephone. This way, I can still hear the "askee's" voice and don't have to fret over the e-mail hoping that the "when pigs fly" remark was merely sarcasm.

The nerve-wracking task of asking a boy to Swirl has made me appreciate what, historically, boys have to go deal with. I have also come upon another advantage to having a good group of friends - the "scope-out." It's nice to have pals who will slyly check out the situation to see if that certain someone I have in mind has already been asked.

And while many in the student body had their minds on the date, the dress, and the dance this week, many were focused on what wasn't happening. Dakota Johnson, one of our very own Streaks, passed away last week after battling cancer. Although I did not have the privilege of meeting him, it was obvious that Dakota had many friends who were saddened by his absence in the hallways.

So, as the magic of Swirl unfolds on Saturday night, nervous girls will order salads at dinner, tense guys will prick their fingers on their corsages, and all but the most wallflower of couples will kick off their dress shoes and bust a move on the hardwood of Thiel Gym. And, in the midst of all, date or not, there will definitely be a number of girls saving a dance for that special someone, Dakota Johnson. "Print!" That's a wrap.

Valentine's Day Brightens Otherwise Drab Month

FEBRUARY 17

- -

FEBRUARY, THE TIME OF YEAR WHEN EVERYTHING SEEMS COLD, GRAY and just plain drab. You know it's pretty mundane when the most exciting part of your week is waiting to see if a groundhog named Phil can see his shadow on the ground. All I have to say is, thank goodness for Valentine's Day!

This Wednesday, the stark snow and bleak sky were merely an invisible backdrop for the peppy shades of pink and red that were punctuating the hallways of GHS. While the largest display of these holiday colors could be found soaking in water on the end of long stems, other less visible ones were hidden away inside sealed envelopes.

When I woke up on the morning of the 14th, a humorous card and a few presents from my parents greeted me on the kitchen counter. Included in the gifts was a pair of fire engine red flats my mom had picked out, the perfect lead-in to the coolest part of Valentine's Day. The night before, I put together a special "V-Day" outfit that featured a heart necklace, heart earrings, a retro Barbie shirt, and to top it off … my shiny red flats. Talk about holiday spirit!

It's always fun to see how the creative side of some people springs to life during the "Holiday of Love." Personally, I can't think of anything better than a homemade present. Just knowing that someone spent time and effort for my benefit is a gift itself. Perhaps the most unique present was one received by a friend of mine from her boyfriend Matt. The gift did not come wrapped in a box but involved some thinking that was more "outside the box." Matt and a couple buds pooled their resources and rented the Orpheum for two hours. Here's the awesome kicker. Each boy blindfolded his girlfriend and surprised her with a private showing of the real-life movie "Cinderella Man."

Holidays like Valentine's Day are great "pick-me-ups" throughout dismal times of the year. Sunday will be yet another opportunity to beat the blahs with the celebration of the Chinese New Year, officially kicking off the "Year of the Pig"! Clearly, February is an outstanding month with more to offer than single-digit temps and drab curb appeal. With a shadowy groundhog on one end, a celebrated pig on the other and a lot of love between, who could ask for anything more?

Curse those Nasty 5-Letter Words

FEBRUARY 24

- -

SOMEONE ONCE TOLD ME THERE ARE TWO BASIC RULES FOR A HAPPY life. Rule number one: Don't sweat the small stuff. Rule number two: It's all small stuff.

Walking down the hallways of GHS, I'm an occasional witness to the use of some rather colorful four-letter words. Recently, I have discovered that many five-letter words should be avoided as well. Take "sweat" for example.

They say exercise is good for the mind, body and spirit. I agree! Running used to seem like a chore, but the exhilaration at the end of a two-mile jog always leaves me feeling refreshed. The only downside of exercise is its nasty sidekick ... sweat. Whenever I hit the gym, I bring along music to keep me pumped, especially when I'm running, so I can jog with the beat and block out the sweat.

Another foul five-letter word to beware of is "worry." Worry comes in many forms, not just warts. Making the team, getting good grades, hoping I don't have broccoli in my teeth, and catching the eye of Mr. Dreamy are all things to worry about. And when Mr. Worry reaches his boiling point, he expands into his six-letter cousin, "stress." This guy is the last person I want knocking on my door. Stress is a grim adjective. Stress headaches, stress fractures, stress lines and stressed-out. I suppose stress is the trade-off for being involved in lots of activities.

The best way to pull the welcome mat out from under cousin Stress is to call on my five-letter hero, Captain "Sleep." My favorite long lost friend is feather-filled, cotton covered and made in Japan. I knew it was meant to be with the first feel of my fluffy companion at Bed, Bath and Beyond. Unfortunately, with stacks of homework, early student council meetings, and late-night pep band games, we haven't been in contact enough in recent weeks. Thank goodness for snow days and national holidays such as Presidents' Day that put Captain Sleep to work.

Although my life may seem hectic at times, it's important for me to remember that sweat, stress and worry are self-inflicted. When my brain turns to overload and I hear that knock on my door, it's necessary to remind myself that no matter what's on the other side, it's all small stuff. So just chill out and smile (another great five-letter word)!

Perseverance Pays, In All Life's Endeavors

MARCH 3

- -

JANE, YOUR WORD IS "PERSEVERANCE."

"Perseverance, ahem, P-U-R-S-E-R-V-I-R-E-N-S-E," I boasted into the microphone in front of all my Silas Willard Elementary School teachers and peers. I was in fifth place and victory seemed so close I could almost touch it. Then came that sound, that annoying, heart-wrenching and humiliating screech of the "incorrect" buzzer.

My eyes and heart dropped to the floor. I couldn't bear to look at the other competitors who, just moments before, I had imagined crying as I grinned at my first-place ribbon. As I slumped off the stage, grabbed my backpack and made the lonely walk home, I thought of everyone to blame for my loss except me.

Now that I'm older and it's still tough to spell, I've learned that perseverance really is crucial in life and not only when it comes to spelling bees. As I've said many times before, running has never been my cup of tea. In sixth grade, I ran the mile race in track. I also participated in the shot put, but I won't open that can of worms. It seemed that no matter how fast I ran and how far ahead I started out, I was always the last person to cross the finish line. It wasn't necessarily that I was a horrible runner, it's just that everyone else was faster!

With the dreaded nightmares of track behind me, I entered high school soccer with excitement and a positive "mile-free" mindset. Then came the first day of winter training and the news that buckled my knees. All hope seemed forever lost when I heard the news of the mandatory two-mile run. In order to be marked as finished, we had to run it under

15 minutes. I thought about ways to get around it, but deep down I knew there was no getting past it and that eventually I would have to face my fears. My best freshman year time was 15:24, not good enough.

As a sophomore, the first day of soccer started off with six laps, one mile, around the top floor. Every other day a lap was added. Hats off to whoever came up with this idea of gradually adding the laps to make it easier on people like me.

Before I or my legs knew it, we had made it up to 12 laps and D-Day had arrived faster than I had hoped. With my heart in my throat and a stopwatch in coach's hand, I was off at "GO" like Forrest Gump running across Greenbow County. I sprinted the last lap with my mind and legs on autopilot. Memories of track meets and spelling bees where I'd come so close to meeting my goal came flooding back. I wasn't paying any attention to the names of those who had beat the clock until I heard the one that always turns my head.

With the grin of a spelling bee champ, I heard the words of my freshman year coach echoing in my mind, "Perseverance, Jane." My word had entered my life yet again, except this time around, it saved me.

Guilt the Perfect Cure for Phony Flu

MARCH 10

- -

IF I HAD A DIME FOR EVERY TIME I FOOLED MY PARENTS INTO BELIEVing I was too sick to go to school, I'd have one lonely coin in my pocket. Studies have shown that faking sick is one of the most popular techniques employed by high school students to get out of class. Though it may be the most popular, it isn't always the most successful.

Ferris Bueller made it look like a snap with his sly "too sick" gimmicks, but he had the advantage of being a Hollywood actor. For those like myself, improvising a simple cough, sneeze or even a wheeze can be challenging. There's a fine line between being dramatically convincing and convincingly dramatic. Falling on the floor in "anguish" crosses the line of believability; however, a distinct sniffle every 40 to 50 seconds appears quite realistic. Talking like I've got a stuffy nose has always proven tried and true for me over the years as well.

As convincing as a sore throat may sound, the only repercussion I'll receive is a bag of honey-lemon Halls. Then there is the biggest hurdle to securing that extra day to study for my big test in history, the thermometer. This is where the great invention of the light bulb comes into play. I grab the thermometer and while my parents are outside a five-yard radius, its to the light bulb for the thermometer. I usually remove the instrument once it reaches about 101 degrees, any higher and it may result in an unnecessary run to the doctor! Useful as it may seem, this method of trickery has been forever banned since the "Accidental Mercury Explosion of 1999" when I held the thermometer on the light for a little too long.

Even though I have more tricks up my sleeve than fingers, believe it or not, I've had (knock on wood), perfect attendance all year. Thanks to a little something called "conscience," the most difficult part of executing my "stay home plan" has been the guilt trip back to bed. Once victory is mine, I will feel bad for fibbing to my parents who would, unknowingly, fib to the school when calling me in sick. Dizzying images of stacks of make-up work haunting me for days inspire me to experience a miraculous healing, and then off to school to face the history test (not so bad after all). Thanks for the light bulb idea anyway, Mr. Edison!

Dodgeball Combines Fashion, Fear, Reflexes

MARCH 17

- -

THE SIMPLICITY OF THE GAME IS BEAUTIFUL. NO FANCY EQUIPMENT, no complex rules, no brain-bending strategies. Just take a little red ball and try to smack the opponent upside the head when he isn't looking. And, most importantly, try not to be the smackee!

Information gleaned from Google has it that dodgeball originated in World War II when it was used by the Germans to keep their pilots active and limber as well as improve their hand-eye coordination. The game, or some close form of it, has been labeled with some rather politically incorrect monikers over the years. These include elimination, maulball, murderball and my favorite, bombardment. Fortunately, modern dodgeball rules call for no head-shots, but those of us who can still feel the throbbing left by unforgiving rubber smacking against our exposed flesh understand these labels. No matter where it was established, anyone that has ever tried to bob and weave his way to safety through a dodgeball court has put his social and physical life on the line. There's a reason that early twentieth century dodgeballers referred to the sphere as the "Death Brick."

Spring dodgeball tournaments started this week at GHS with students and teachers lacing those sneakers and heating up their throwing arms at the fierce competition ... each other.

So, after a windy soccer practice Wednesday night, I headed over to Wicall Gymnasium, home of the "dodgeballers" themselves to get a sense of how a real match goes down. Peering in, I noticed the gym was separated into four courts by giant curtains that hung from the ceiling. The size of the playing fields was less intimidating than I had imagined. The few bystanders there stood along the sidelines out of the line of fire. Of course, an occasional wayward ball would come my way but that's the price to pay for floor seats.

Being the wanna-be "fashionista" that I am, I took note of each player's attire. A couple of teams made T-shirts while others coordinated their gym clothes with goofy knee socks and sweatbands. I could see for some it was a competition to see who could dress the funkiest, not who could pummel the most opponents. Another point of interest, and perhaps most humorous, were some of the team names. A team of boastful teachers called themselves "The Untouchables." Other comical names such as "The Wheezing Geezers," "Dancing Nancies," and "Creampuffs" are what set this extracurricular apart from the others.

The game moved fast, and it appeared there were basically two kinds of players, the quick and the "dead." While everyone was having much fun, I felt great sympathy for the final remaining player on each team, especially when it was one versus three or four! At that point, I'd come up with one more name for dodgeball: "See Jane Run, See Jane Run Fast!"

Lunch Snacks Get Boot to Help Kids

MARCH 24

- -

DURING LUNCH, MY SPARE CHANGE USUALLY ENDS UP IN THE BANK of the Snack Square for a Laffy Taffy or pack of Starburst. But this week, my dollar bills went sugarless and were put toward a much more significant, selfless cause.

St. Jude's is a non-profit children's research hospital known for its work in finding a cure and saving the lives of kids with pediatric cancer and other terminal illnesses. It was only a matter of time before another great organization dedicated to helping others, the GHS Student Council, found a way to pitch in.

What high school student doesn't love a good challenge every now and then, other than math homework? In order to get everyone hyped up for the St. Jude's donations, the council made 1,000 little paper feet that students and staff could buy for $1 each. Each paper foot gets the donor's name written on it so others can see how their contributions really make a difference.

All the feet are then posted up starting at one wall and trailing around the lower square of the high school until they wrap back around to the starting line. Members of student council walk from table to table with the donation can and sell the paper feet during each lunch period.

Late this week, my friend Jenna and I paraded through the lunchroom armed with the can for donations and a manila folder packed with paper feet. Much to our joy and surprise, several students left their tables and came to us with their donations. Our teachers also stepped up to the plate and were very generous in their contributions as well. By the end of Thursday, it was obvious that reaching our goal wouldn't be a problem with the foot race already making the turn down the history hallway.

Selling the feet has also taken care of much needed spring-cleaning. Leftover T-shirts from Homecoming, Swirl and Battle of the Bands have been crowding the student council office for months. In order to solve this pesky problem, donors receive their pick of one of these T-shirts for every four feet purchased.

While the free T-shirt is a bargain, my favorite incentive is how it connects me with others across the nation by reaching out to them with a helping hand, or in this case, foot.

Writer Finds Inspiration in Reading Others

MARCH 31

- -

MY MIND IS A BARREN DESERT AS I STARE AT THE BLANK WORD DOCument on my computer screen. It's Thursday night, closing in on 10 p.m. I just returned home from a victorious soccer game and the only thing I want to focus on is the inside of my eyelids.

I search my mind trying to find a subject, but my creativity box is locked for the night and the key is nowhere to be found. It seems like every time I set fingertips to keyboard, the cursor refuses to budge.

Writer's block is an illness that often tricks me into believing there really is no cure. Whenever I hit a dead end on the roads of writing, I follow my own prescription: stop, drop and read.

On the occasion that I'm trying to come up with an article about athletics, I swallow two large columns from Sports Illustrated magazine. Reading a story about a championship game transcends my mind into an intense and competitive atmosphere. Words such as "fierce" and "intense" start connecting with each other like pieces to a puzzle and before I know it, I'm on a roll.

Then there are the times when my daily life seems bland and the only cure is a good laugh. This is where the Sunday comics come into play. In my 15 and a half years of humor experience, I know I can never go wrong with a good "For Better or Worse" or a little "Peanuts" every now and then to get me in a quirky, artistic mood.

For the more heartfelt columns, I bring my sensitive side out by brushing up on excerpts from the "Chicken Soup for the Soul" series. The "Chicken Soup" stories are basically heart-warming or heart-wrenching, true tales of the experiences of people across America. These types of articles are the easiest for me to write because they always speak from the soul rather than the mind.

The clock has struck midnight and any idea at this point would be utterly miraculous. Maybe my mind is telling me it's time for plan B, another trusty anecdote for "The Big Block" - a good night's rest. Good Night, Moon.

Sweet 16: Dating, Driving, and a Bassoon Serenade

APRIL 7

- -

"SIXTEEN CANDLES" MOANED ITS MELODY IN THE BACKGROUND. A sea of my adoring guests broke it down on the dance floor as Justin Timberlake crooned "Happy Birthday" to me. And just when this magical night couldn't possibly get any better, my parents surprised me with a fiery red BMW that was so shiny even my reflection had a reflection.

And that's when the cheering of my entourage turned out to be just my mom reciting another chapter of her favorite novel, "Jane's Chores."

I suppose most teenagers would love the thought of an extravagant, blowout party for their own Sweet 16, but in my eyes, less is more.

Don't get me wrong, I love celebrating my big day with friends, but I'd rather enjoy the company of a few close pals than be packed in a room with hundreds of guests I don't even know. I can't imagine the amount of thank you notes I would have to write! Instead of Mr. Timberlake drooling into the microphone, I'd just as soon have a celebratory rendition by Clark, my fellow Silver Streaks bassoonist. As far as the fiery red BMW goes, make that a blue one. My practicality only goes so far.

When I wake up Sunday morning, there will likely be no chocolate Easter bunnies or marshmallow Peeps waiting for me downstairs. At church, my mind will be focused on the message instead of occasionally doodling on the back of the collection envelope, and later in the afternoon I will be officially promoted from "finder" to "hider" at the big Easter Egg Hunt at Grandma's.

Because this Sunday, my family will not only be rejoicing in honor of the Easter holiday, but commemorating the 16th anniversary of my birth. Though I'm sure this coincidence has no profound religious or chronological meaning, it does make the day twice as special for me.

Speaking of being officially promoted, two new doors have been unlocked with the liberating 16 key. I am legally allowed to date and drive. The latter one permitted by the state of Illinois and the former one permitted by my parents.

This is my last column as a 15-year old sophomore; does this mean the final chapter of "Jane's Chores" has been written? Probably not. But I'm looking forward to a great day anyway. Oh, and before I forget - Clark, if you're reading this, don't forget your bassoon on Sunday!

Shopping Sounds Better than Bleeding

APRIL 14

REMEMBER THE HOT-SHOT KIDS WHO SLID INTO FIRST BASE DURING P.E. just so they could show off their battle scars later?

Well, let's just say I was the exact antithesis of them. Remember me? I was the outfielder most likely to dive away from fly balls rather than for them, and so I stuck to braiding daisies instead.

Also, I was the only one on my team to strike out in kickball and my favorite part of dodgeball is the dodge. Sad to say, I am a flincher at times. The fear of pain has always been my weakness.

This weakness was almost put to the test when student council announced sign-ups for the annual blood drive. Every year at GHS, students at least 16 years old can donate their blood to the American Red Cross. Once collected and processed, the blood helps those in desperate need of it, such as victims of a bad accident or those who are undergoing critical surgery.

Being big on charities, I signed up to donate. The only snag I didn't foresee at the time, or maybe just didn't want to see, was the whole "giving blood" part. To this day, I still need to be bribed into getting a shot at the doctor's office. Stickers, lollipops, whatever can distract me from that frightful needle.

As donation time grew nearer, remorse shadowed me like an unwelcomed guest and stress came on so heavily I thought I was carrying bricks in my backpack. I felt like I was back in P.E. class again, running to the back of the batting line to avoid stepping up to the plate and facing that cowhide in the kisser.

I was relieved of the weight of worry, however, when I realized I would be able to give a donation in a different, less prickly, way. The homecoming carnival was moved to this spring and during the event, there will be a silent auction. The highest bid money will go toward reaching our $1,000 goal for the St. Jude's Foundation. Now I may not be the most aggressive player on the field, but when it comes to shopping or just spending money in general, I'm your girl.

So even though it won't be in blood, I feel good inside knowing that my actions can still help make the quality of someone's life better or hopefully prolong a life hanging in the balance. Gee, I wonder what the highest bid is on those elbow pads?

Soccer Match Kicks Up Some Life Lessons

APRIL 21

- -

WHAT A GAME IT WAS! WITH THE POTENTIAL CONFERENCE CROWN AT stake, the intensity was immense and every one of my teammates showcased her drive for the game at every chance. It was a well-fought match and, after two scoreless 10-minute overtimes, the final tally of 1-1 proved it.

While there was no "thrill of victory" being displayed by either team following the Streaks' soccer match with the Moline Maroons on Thursday, the 100 minutes of scoreboard deadlock did produce plenty of "agony of da feet" for those who had left it all on the field.

Though it was a fantastic game, it's always a spirit-lifter to come out on top. As Vince Lombardi, the great Packers coach put it, "winning isn't everything, its the only thing." Nobody enjoys losing, unless you're dieting.

Taken literally, however, I find that sets me up for a lot of sadness. I prefer, "You don't have to win, to win." Similar words of wisdom came from our coaches during the post-game talk following this key Western Big 6 matchup. Soccer has taught me more than how to kick a ball, in fact, many of the things I've learned over this season can be applied to daily life. Just like Thursday's game with Moline, it is the dogged pursuit of getting that "A" in geometry or finding the perfect prom dress that really matters.

Before every game, we're told to "own the first 10 minutes." In layman's terms, if we can keep possession of the ball and play Streaks soccer for the first critical minutes, it will set the tone for the first half and ultimately the entire game. I've related this instruction with the beginning of the school year or semester when I'm just getting into the swing of things. It is this time that is most crucial as I predetermine my success and attitude throughout the term. This philosophy also applies to each individual day. Getting up on the right side of the bed and starting with a good hair day always helps put me on the path to a successful day.

"Every 60 seconds in a game, ask yourself if you're where you need to be," yet another applicable concept of Silver Streaks soccer. This lesson relates more on a personal level than anything. Occasionally, I must take note of where I'm at, where I'm going, and the paths I need to follow in order to achieve goals.

So, soccer goals, life's goals, it doesn't matter. Listen to your "coaches." Every so often, one of those pearls of wisdom will ultimately net you not only soccer balls, but other successes down life's road.

No Sun Required for Job Shadows

APRIL 28

- -

THOUGH THE SUN WASN'T OUT ON WEDNESDAY MORNING, THERE was still a cast of shadows created by students at GHS. Wednesday was not a typical school day. Rather than throwing on the usual T-shirt and jeans before sliding on my sneakers, I buttoned up a crisp blouse and donned a pair of black capri pants. Learning about the Germans' role in World War I was set aside for the day in favor of a modern, behind the scenes look at the inner-workings of a local retail store.

Job Shadow Day is open to all sophomores and seniors interested in learning about a particular career, including a wide array of professions from firefighter to undercover cop, interior designer to outdoor landscaper. Being a sophomore, I was completely oblivious as of what to expect.

Included in the sign-up sheet was a resume in which I answered questions such as, "What hobbies do you enjoy, what activities are you involved in, and most importantly, what volunteer work have you been a part of?" I never realized some of the jobs on the list of workplaces even existed.

With such a broad selection, it was tough to settle on one career, but eventually I narrowed my suspects down to two, Fashion Design and Radio Broadcasting. Based upon these choices, it was decided where and whom I would be shadowing on the big day. Fittingly, I ended up at the mall, where I got a feel for what it's like to manage a large department store. Spending a few hours with Mrs. Langerman, store manager at JCPenney, really opened my eyes to the hard work that goes into the job and how many people it takes to make things happen. I was surprised to learn the employees at the local store did not actually get to select its merchandise. I suppose this happens at a higher JCPenney location. I enjoyed the experience, which will have payoffs on future shopping trips there.

Perhaps the most exciting part of Job Shadow Day was hearing the feedback from everyone else's experience. My friend Matt, an aspiring chef, was taken to a Galesburg restaurant called "Q's Cafe." Not only did he meet the business owners and get some hands-on experience with customers and a few recipes, but he also received a special Q's lunch, packed for when he got back to school.

Melinda, another pal, took a trip over to Burgland Drug and spent a couple hours with the pharmacist, Mr. Burgland himself. She noted how busy he was and the personal touches he had with the customers. My bud Jordan spent the day at the Knox County Nursing Home, while Sarah, who aspires to be a teacher someday, saw a classroom from the other side when she shadowed at Gale Elementary School.

It was a fun and interesting day that was sponsored by the Rotary Club. With all the exciting careers on the list, maybe we should make this a weekly event?

Who are You? Call her Janey Depp

MAY 5

- -

THEY CALL ME "SIMMY" ON THE SOCCER FIELD, "JANERS" IN THE hallways, and on the home front it's "Mayor of Sassy City." Nicknames - they're simple but useful, catchy yet personal.

Walking into the classroom of Mrs. Wiley-Parkin (also known as "Mrs. W.P"), I would never have guessed I would be walking out with a new identity. Well, at least during first block. Every now and then, Mrs. W.P will dub one of her pupils with her own nickname usually taking after a unique personality trait. For "Dress Like Your Favorite Celebrity Day," I threw on some pearls, a black shirt, black straight-leg pants, and flats for the Audrey Hepburn look. Ever since that day, I've been referred to as "Audrey" when it's my turn to read in front of the class or answer a question.

For many folks, nicknames are obvious and fit like a glove. Take for instance, "The Seven Dwarfs" who were each named after his own peculiar mannerism. Sneezy, Sleepy, Grumpy, Bashful, and who could forget Dopey.

Occasionally, a nickname will be replaced with a "pet name." I'm not talking about Rover or Spot next door. Pet names tend be more, how shall I say, "lovey-dovey." These terms of endearment can range anywhere from "Honey Bun" to "Sugar Pie." If it sounds like it could cause a cavity, it's most likely a pet name. However, on a more literal note, if someone calls out "Boo" at my friend Jenna's house, both her and her cat's ears will perk up! Being nicknamed after the family pet can be a bit confusing at times. Just ask Indiana (named after his dog) Jones.

Nicknames are handy as well, especially if I'm in a big city and lost my mom in a sea of people or if I'm subbing in for someone on the soccer field. Something short, but unique enough to grab your attention, like "C.C." rather than the whole "Cynthia," proves to be beneficial in many situations, especially if you're trying to fit it on a license plate or the back of a team shirt.

My favorite kind of nicknames are those that I've shared among my friends that bring back great memories. In junior high, I called my friend Katie "Moose," and as a play on the terms "Jane Doe" and "John Deere" she designated me as "Jane Deer." The nicknames went along with our handshake where we bucked "antlers" rather than the traditional high-five.

In the future, I see my nickname taking on a rather star-like quality - can you say, Mrs. Johnny Depp?

Thanks, Mom!

MAY 12

- -

MOTHERS, THIS ONE'S FOR YOU.

Being a teenager myself, I realize we tend to think the world revolves around us. Rarely do we show our appreciation for those who take time from their lives to help us manage our own. So, here's my gift to you, Mom, and other moms around the world, some personal recognition by my fellow GHS classmates and me.

"Thank you for packing my lunch for me since the kindergarten days. No matter how old I get, I'll never be able to master chef a PB and J quite like yours." - Love, Jane

"Thank you for inspiring me to be the person I am today." - Emma

"Thanks for teaching me that family comes first, but math home-work is sometimes a close second." - Love, Sam

"Thank you for always being there when I need you and believing in me in everything I do." - Matt

"Thank you for teaching me to be the best person I can be and for always supporting me. I love you!" - Emma

"Thanks for always being there no matter what I needed. You truly are my hero." - Love, Jenna

"Thank you for raising me to be the person I am and teaching me that the greatest gift is family." - Brandon

"Thank you, Mom! I know that I'm not always perfect but you try so hard so I can have a perfect life. Thank you again, Mom!" - Love, Mitchel

"Thanks for teaching me it's all right to splurge on a pair of cute shoes ... as long as Dad doesn't find out! I love you!" - Alexa

"Thanks for making our home a landmark for the world's best cheesecake!" - Maria

"Thanks for always being my number one fan in life." - Love, Lindsay

"Thanks for always being there to cheer me up and for being the best Kool-Aid mom ever!" - Love, Peter

This Saturday I'll be participating in the Susan G. Komen "Race for the Cure" in Peoria along with my friend Alexa and her grandmother. Mothers, daughters, grandmothers, sisters, aunts, and nieces will hit the pavement early in the morning for a 5-kilometer walk in support of the search for ending breast cancer. To all the mom figures out there, I lift up my PB and J (made with an extra layer of love) to you. Happy Mother's Day!

Driver's Ed More than Stop and Go

MAY 19

WHEN I WAS YOUNGER, MY FRIENDS AND I USED TO PLAY A GAME called "Red Light, Green Light" in the driveway on our roller blades. One person would call out "green light!" and we would go as far as we could until they said, "red light!" Whoever reached the finish line first was declared the champion and won a stick of gum.

When I received the "Rules of the Road" book for my driver's ed test, I was a little overwhelmed when "starting and stopping" weren't the only subjects in the index. Roadway signs, traffic laws and pavement markings were circling my mind like a bat caught in a bedroom after trying to absorb as much information as I could to prepare for my permit test. If anyone ever needs to know how to change a spare tire, I'm ... working on it.

This Wednesday, it was time for me to put my driving knowledge to the test. Missing more than 12 questions would result in disqualification for the coveted permit. Much to my relief, I didn't score as dreadfully as I had dreamt. Those wicked nightmares of evil test scores chasing me down gloomy hallways were finally put to rest.

The only worry racking my brain now is the actual driving part of driver's education, which I am signed up for this summer. Four-way stops and I have never been great friends. Whenever I pull up to one while riding my bike, I pedal down the street and wait to cross out of someone's driveway. For some reason I highly doubt my teacher will allow me to perform my usual ritual of skipping the intersection. Who knows? Maybe I'll learn to become at one with the four-way stop and the next time I ride my bike I won't have to wait for someone to honk at me to know when to cross.

Then there's this infamous "chicken brake" I've been hearing so much about from all the driver's ed veterans. Supposedly there's not one, but two brake pedals in the driver's ed cars, one for the student driver and one for the teacher. Whenever the teacher feels it's necessary to stop, he or she can put the brakes on at any moment, in some cases, causing a mild whiplash to those in the back seat.

While other students are ruthlessly hitting the snooze button during the first few weeks of summer vacation, I'll be wide-eyed behind the wheel. Some of my friends will be blasting their stereos to the Top 20 countdown while I tune the car radio searching for the traffic reports. However, I've got a feeling all this studying will pay off, possibly on a nice summer day when I slap on my skates for a pick-up game of "Red Light, Green Light." I hope my friends come prepared with lots of Double Bubble!

She's Leaving the Band, But Not the Music

MAY 26

- -

MUSIC IS LIKE AN OLD FRIEND I'VE KNOWN ALL MY LIFE. IT LETS ME vent my frustrations and is always there for me when I need it. If I'm in a bad mood, I can always pound the piano to a powerful piece by Beethoven, while a quick blast of good ol' "Hi-Ho Silver!" on my mellophone is the ticket for getting me pumped and focused for a big game.

My two years participating in the Galesburg High School band program have built strong bonds with new friends, a powerful work ethic, and most importantly, confidence in being who I am. Sadly, this Memorial Day parade, I will strut my final steps down Main Street as a Galesburg Marching Streak. However, you can bet I'll be leaving with more than just a mean right flank.

If I had a dollar for all of the funny moments and good times I've shared with my fellow band mates, I could buy my own bassoon! Bus rides to competitions, the ever-so-popular band camp, pep band games, concerts - I could talk for days about all the great memories I've collected over the past two years.

One moment I'll never forget is the first time we won grand champion at a competition my freshman year. Kids were jumping up and down as if their shoes were pogo sticks and high-fives were handed out like candy at Halloween. Witnessing over 150 of my friends working toward, then achieving, the same goal left me with an indescribable feeling of pride. The looks of gratification on our directors' faces were quite priceless as well.

To the inexperienced eye, marching around and playing an instrument may seem like an easy task. That's where you'd be wrong. First off, at the beginning of a parade or field competition the entire band is called to a position of "attention." Attention means absolutely no moving or talking, keeping the chin up, eyes forward, and putting on Mr. Stone Face. It's hard enough keeping a class of 20 teenagers from bouncing off the classroom walls, let alone keeping 180 on task outdoors on a steamy August day! If people still don't believe me, then I challenge them to pick up a 5-pound textbook and hold it up and out in front of them, staying frozen in that position for two to three minutes. I never even knew I had triceps until my first couple weeks of band camp.

Next fall will bring new challenges and experiences with my junior year, but I will be seeing less of that old friend of mine in the west hall of GHS. Luckily for me, I'll always know where to find her should I need an occasional pick-me-up. That's at halftime on Van Dyke Field, during timeouts in the bleachers of Thiel Gym, inside my trumpet case in the corner of my room, or just anytime I need her in the most treasured recesses of my memory. "Hi-Ho Silver - Away!"

What Will Summer Bring? June in Here in August

JUNE 2

THIS TIME OF THE YEAR, TV SHOWS ARE ENDING THEIR SEASONS WITH cliffhangers to keep viewers anxious for the fall episodes. Too often, we are left with the main character's life hanging in the balance or an unexpected marriage proposal comes out of nowhere. Will Pam and Jim finally get together on "The Office"? Did desperate housewife Edie really do herself in or was that some other desperate soul's feet dangling in midair? Will Lassie get Timmy out of the well?

Personally, I don't see a marriage proposal in my near future and hopefully my life won't be hanging in any balances, but there are some slightly less dramatic cliffhangers for me at the end of this school year.

Take Driver's Ed. Who will be my brave, unfortunate, behind-the-wheel teacher? Will I be able to make turns without cuffing the curb or a squirrel? How many times will my instructor be forced to hit the chicken break? And when, if ever, will my parents trust me with manning the wheel of the family truckster?

Speaking of the family, during August, the Simkins gang will be heading up north to "rough it" in the great outdoors of the Boundary Waters Canoe Area. Now, I've heard that bears tend to hang around the campsites at night and your food bag has to be hung from a tree. Will I learn how to run at a faster pace or at least quick enough to pass my dad? Will my mom find peace in listening to loons under the stars or will she be dreaming of the featherbed at the Country Inn and Suites? And, most importantly, will I be able to survive with nothing to fall asleep to but the droning snores of my older brother and the Minnesota Mosquito Ensemble?

With the summer season also comes golf practices, meets, and tournaments. Thus, a substantial amount of my summer will be spent on the greens. If you're at the course this year and you hear a "FORE!" either someone had a good hole or I'm nearby. Could this be the year I dig my golf game out of the sandtrap and onto the fairway?

I'm sure my parents are wondering if I'll ever get that summer job I've been promising them for about a month now. Will you see me at the drive-through window at your favorite restaurant? Or perhaps I'll be the one mowing your lawn twice a week?

Although my August will be a bit less busy without Band Camp, I'm sure it will fill quickly with some of the new activities and courses that I had previously not had time to try. Perhaps my dog Boomer and I will find a more regular exercise pattern to shed some of his sitting around pounds.

Whatever the outcome of the summer, I'll be sure to fill you in during the next season of Jane's Journal! Thanks to all for your nice comments and here's hoping that all your cliffhangers find you pulling yourself back on top of the mountain and enjoying the view. Have a great summer!

JUNIOR YEAR

Driving Through the Summer and Back to School

AUGUST 25

- -

It didn't hit me when I signed my medical release forms at registration. It didn't hit me when I dug numerous flyers for school supplies out of our mailbox. And when I first reviewed my class schedule, I never thought twice about how soon I'd be back at GHS.

Not until I received a "welcome back" letter from my American Studies teachers did reality strike me like a ruler. In a few days, I'd be passing through those familiar band hallway doors, but this time with upperclassman status.

In my last column in May, I proclaimed about embarking on a "summer of firsts" - including my first time behind the wheel of a car that didn't kick on with two Happy Joe's tokens. I also received my first permit. And I've still got bug bites from my first time camping, outside of my back yard. It was an exciting summer to say the least.

The first week of driver's ed felt like jumping off the high dive without knowing how to swim. It was only my second day of class when I was given my permit and my first shot behind the wheel. Through a series of "chicken brakes," wrong turns and aimless Sunday drives, I'm pain-stakingly collecting my 50, behind the wheel hours towards earning my license.

Another grand adventure over the break was roughing it for five days with my family in the Boundary Waters. Trekking through the wilderness with an 80-pound pack strapped to my back, I realized how lugging all those books around has really paid off!

I'm encouraged that that my summer driving skills will help me land a space in our freshly paved parking lot at GHS and that my August paddling will continue through my junior year, making it a bit easier to understand the importance of a high-carb diet to sustain energy. I just hope the cafeteria stocks plenty of bagels and trail mix.

Ode to a Canvas Companion

SEPTEMBER 1

- -

I WOULD LIKE TO DEDICATE THIS JOURNAL ENTRY TO A DEAR FRIEND of mine, one who has been with me through it all.

She was there on my first day of high school, rode with me on numerous bus trips with the soccer team, and stuck with me on occasional mad dashes from the parking lot to an early morning student council meeting. Even though I only catch glimpses of you during summer vacations, I know we'll always be able to pick up where we left off once school rolls around again.

Backpack, this one's for you.

As you lay limp like a deflated hot air balloon staring back at me from the wooden chair, I begin reminiscing about the first time we met. Designing you myself from a Web site (www.NikeID.com), I had the privilege of expressing my love of fashion in my canvas companion. Combining flattering shades of pink and green, adding a splash of navy, and topping it off with my first and middle name proudly embroidered on the pocket, I grinned confidently back at the monitor while waiting anxiously for your arrival. Ten business days later, you showed up on my doorstep and we've been like two peas in a very cute pod ever since.

Backpack, I would like to apologize ahead of time for the stress and strain you will endure this year. Get ready to cinch your straps as junior year is going to challenge both of us. Oh, and don't expect a great deal of free space to hang out in our locker this semester. Advanced biology and American studies projects have already staked their claim. Not to worry, my friend. I've heard I'll be working on exciting assignments in American studies that may include a chance for you to rub elbows with the likes of Abraham Lincoln, F.D.R. and "The Babe." Maybe I'll be able to freshen up your daytime hangout with a bunch of roses from a photosynthesis class in biology.

I realize you may be overwhelmed with the "Grammar and Composition" book. However, there is one downsize this year. Our algebra II teacher has given us the opportunity to use a CD-ROM version of our textbook - how's that for lightening your load.

As I zip you up, allow you to rest up on the kitchen table and prepare for the day ahead, I want to say, "thank you." Thanks for being my pillow on long bus rides or road trips. Thanks for boosting me up so I can toss my lunch bag on the top shelf. And mainly, thanks, pal, for always having my back.

She's Still Got the Music in Her

SEPTEMBER 8

- -

AFTER THE MEMORIAL DAY PARADE LAST MAY, I TURNED IN MY UNIform, closed the lid on my helmet and retired my mellophone; however, the music never left my soul. So, I must admit, standing on the other side of the fence at last Friday's football game felt surreal.

Flashing back to one year ago, I vividly remember standing at parade rest on the rubbery track anticipating the trill of Mr. B's whistle to snap me into attention. I still recall the feeling of pride as we sounded "William Tell" during the pre-game show. The football team charged onto the field and for a moment in time, the Marching Streaks and Silver Streaks football team connected as one force of school pride.

I miss the camaraderie shared with my marching mates, especially the mello section. After two years of inside jokes, drill rehearsals and nerve-wracking marching competitions, the attachment to the band program is not easy to shake. How could I forget my freshman year when the title "Grand Champions" was awarded to our band? Wearing our forest green "Medieval Knights" T-shirts, a celebration began around the

Washington High School track and continued with high fives, hugs and celebratory dances around the fleet of District 205 school buses.

Transitioning from marching to concert took time to adjust, as sitting instead of moving became the focus. Transitioning from the mellophone to bassoon was made easier with Brandon and Rose by my side. Playing along with two hardworking and talented musicians motivated me to become a better bassoonist myself.

Band provided me with a love and appreciation of all types of music. I have returned to playing the piano with a better understanding of melody. It also helps to realize a Sunday afternoon recital is no longer haunting me. My mp3 player has replaced the television when I find a moment of free time to kick back.

On a Friday night, while either sweating in the polyester one-piece or freezing in the stands on a late October night, envy would occasionally take over as I saw my friends cheering or chatting in their own personal style. Now that I have experienced the other side of the fence, I must say the grass is not always greener. Whether I'm marching with the band, or to the beat of my own drum, I will always have the utmost respect for the Marching Streaks. In my own musical world, I'm with the band, no matter what side of the fence I live.

Theme Music Changes with the Moment

SEPTEMBER 15

- -

WHAT IF LIFE WERE ONE BIG MUSICAL? WHAT IF EVERYONE HAD HER own theme song? After watching a rerun of Disney's "High School Musical" for the umpteenth time, I began pondering these questions myself.

I've always wondered what it would be like to walk down the hallway and instantly start strutting to the beat of my own theme song. Of course, the tune would change according to whatever flowed with my mood at the time. For instance, if I were about to tackle an intimidating Algebra II test, I could definitely get pumped up with some "I Will Survive," by Gloria Gaynor. Or, if I fell asleep before studying my biology the night before a final "I Believe in Miracles," by Whitney Houston would also be at the top of my playlist. What about those rare days when I score a perfect on Mrs. Gutzsky's vocabulary test? I'd be the sixth member of the Jackson Five while I jived through the English wing blaring, "A, B, C, it's easy as 1, 2, 3 ...!" But it's not all ballads of glory.

Everyone has a bad test grade now and then. I can see it now; I scuff my feet down the barren halls with Dean Martin adding salt to my wounds, chanting "Ain't that a Kick in the Head." Then again, Dean's old pal Frank Sinatra would back him up with a rendition of "That's Life."

In the intense realm of athletics, classic rock ranging from AC/DC to Led Zeppelin would be set on full blast when I geared up for a soccer game. Heading off to a competitive round of dodgeball, the gym doors would swing open as I strolled into John Thiel gymnasium to the chorus of "Another One Bites the Dust." Teeing off in a golf match, peaceful flutes and violins would fill the air with a focused serenity. No other song but Queen's "We are the Champions" would suit the gratifying feeling of a well-deserved victory.

And how could I forget those ever-so-popular lovey-dovey jingles? Walking to class with that "oh so special someone" we'd become the modern-day Sonny and Cher as we waltzed among the cafeteria tables to "I Got You Babe." This is all hypothetically speaking of course. ...

Johnny Carson had "The Tonight Show" band. Oprah has her own signature "walk out" music. Maybe someda I'll stroll down New York City's Fifth Avenue as an "Uptown Girl," but for now, I'm just a "Brown-Eyed Girl" dreaming of that place where the neon lights are pretty, "Downtown."

Sweet Sensations of Homecoming Week

SEPTEMBER 22

- -

"CANDYLAND" WAS ALWAYS MY FAVORITE BOARD GAME GROWING UP. My brother and I played it so many times that the colorful board began to fade and fray. Much to my surprise and delight, this year's GHS Homecoming theme is "Candyland," and just like the game itself, homecoming week is sure to be an adventure of silliness, excitement and all-around fun.

Perhaps, one of my favorite components of homecoming week is Spirit Wear Days. Who doesn't want an excuse to play dress up every now and then? With a theme based on sugar, how could Student Council resist conjuring up some "sweet" ideas?

Starting off the week and sure to be a grand slam is "Baby Ruth Monday." The catch of this theme is for everyone to strut the halls sporting his or her most beloved baseball team T-shirt.

"Nerds Day" is the one I'm looking forward to the most as it should bring out some unique looks. My friend Caitlin and I have already got our costumes in mind, complete with extra-large rimmed specs, our brothers' suspenders, pocket protectors and "high-water" pants to complete the ensemble.

Other dress up days include "Peppermint Day" with the student body adorned in their best red and white duds, and of course "Spirit Day Friday" where classmates show their pride by donning a Streaks shirt or this year's official Homecoming T-shirt.

The Senior Sweet Tarts and Junior Jawbreakers are the two teams going for the goal in this year's Powder Puff game. Being their first time on the other side of the track, some of my female classmates have been seen sharpening their pigskin skills for the big game. Although it's only flag football, the intensity of the "seniority factor" can give even the fans in the stands that competitive drive.

Then there's the humorous side of Powder Puff - cheering on the sidelines and attempting to create a human pyramid. Cheerleading roles are taken over by the junior and senior guys during the contest and they usually surprise me with their upbeat attitude and thunderous cheers.

Following Wednesday's Powder Puff, the class floats will be presented in the parade on Friday. This will be my first year wearing something other than a band uniform and helmet while passing down Main Street. This year, I'll be riding in golf carts with my teammates Kat and Jorden along with the rest of the Girls Golf team.

Nominations for homecoming court were held this week and the King and Queen will be crowned next Friday. I am also looking forward to the homecoming game itself, as our Streaks will undoubtedly be layin' a little whippin' on those Maroons from Moline. That will most assuredly be the frosting on a sweet homecoming week!

Golf No Sport for the Weak

SEPTEMBER 29

IF I WERE A DICTIONARY, I WOULD DEFINE THE WORD "SLUMP" AS A frustrating period where a person is consistently inconsistent. Thank goodness my last name isn't Webster.

Golf is tough. Even if you're a Wie or a Woods, hitting a slump is inevitable. One of the most frustrating aspects of this sport is that after I seemingly correct one problem with my game, there is another one waiting in the bag.

At the beginning of the GHS season, I referred to my driver as "the chosen club." I was hitting it so well, I once thought about using it as a putter. After a couple of city tournaments, I didn't even think about, let alone play, a round of golf for about a week. This is how I learned the lesson of "practice makes perfect" the hard way. As the fall season got under way, stepping onto that suddenly foreign environment of the first tee box quickly became the dreaded misadventures of Jane. With the swing of the club, the "chosen club" morphed into its evil twin, "the shanky shaft." I stood dumbstruck on No. 1 at Lake Bracken like a deer in the headlights, watching my Titleist 2 disappear into the depths of the timber on the right.

Three years of golf experience has shown me that the best cure for a bad drive is to seek a little help from the pros, namely Coach Gottenborg and Coach Herrin. They graciously help with tweaks and suggestions to lower my score, while the real pro, J.R., is available to help me get the big kinks out of my swing. Often though, I'll just ask my friend (and fellow teammate), "Jorden, what am I doing wrong?!" A few words of golfing wisdom from Jorden and my line of flight is repositioned from the traps to the pin.

Though receiving help from more experienced golfers is a fantastic learning tool, there are situations where I'm forced to correct my game by myself. So far, I've found the key to getting out of a slump on my own is realizing how I got there in the first place. Once I discover the glitch behind the missed putts, blades, hooks and shanks, I take a mental recap on my normal grip and swing, line up the grooves on the club face to the target, take the club inside, swing through at the hole and, most importantly, pray it goes in the right direction.

Over time I am realizing it's not the problem that makes me weaker, it's the hard work and stepping stones I take to climb back up the ladder of par. Golf's tough. Get a helmet.

New Driver Alert: Jane's on the Road!

OCTOBER 6

ATTENTION ALL DRIVERS, DOG WALKERS, CYCLISTS AND PEDESTRI-ans! Jane Simkins now has her driver's license. I repeat, Jane Simkins has her license.

I thought the day would never come. From the time that I was very little, there have been nightmares about driving solo. But with a month of driver's education with great instructors under my belt, those recurring dreams are a thing of the past.

Last Thursday night was my first time manning the wheel without anyone else on board. No parent reminding me to slow down, cover the brake and get on my side of the street. After some stall tactics, like adjusting the rear-view mirror 10 times, I started the engine on the family Buick. With a shaky death grip on the wheel, I backed out of the driveway like a turtle wading through quicksand. My CDs provided minimal relaxation as I focused intensely on the road laid out before me. Pulling, or rather creeping, up to the first four-way stop at Fremont Street, my eyes were pingpong balls darting cautiously from left to right to left.

Upon reaching the intimidating Henderson-Fremont intersection, a haunting driver's ed video on wrecks came flashing back to mind. In a state of fear, I began to panic. What if that driver across the way is totally oblivious to me and I get side-swiped? What if the Rendezvous suddenly decides to die the second the light turns green? How do I turn on the hazard lights? Am I registered on the insurance for the Buick yet? For a brief moment, I was even debating whether or not to call the folks at OnStar for advice on getting out of this impending predicament.

Instinctively, something inside me took control of the situation. Predicament? Wait a minute, what predicament was I in? Reassuring myself of the month of driver's ed and 50 hours of permit time I had logged over the summer, my grip began to loosen a little on the steering wheel. Eventually, the light turned green and I made my way with a hint of confidence down Fremont Street to the high school. Upon performing a flawless, between the lines parking maneuver, I exited the Buick with no injuries or call to OnStar.

My confidence continues to build with each solo journey to watch a soccer game or work on a class project. My parents no longer coach me from the driveway with fake smiles hiding their obvious panic. Independence, however, will take a back seat when traveling to school, as my lifelong friend, Emily, will continue to drive me to the school parking lot. Although I may not be able to drive anywhere, any time, the newly-found freedom of a license was well worth the 50-hour wait.

See you on the road!

Procrastination a Skill Worth Perfecting

OCTOBER 13

HESITANTLY, I LOOK TOWARD THE CLOCK AT THE BOTTOM OF THE computer screen. 11 p.m. Ouch.

I could have started my five-page term paper last Monday when I was given the assignment in Grammar and Comp. I could have begun studying for my American Studies test a few days ago when I circled the date in my agenda. I also could have worked on getting my Algebra II notes organized for the homework quiz tomorrow. What can I say? I'm just a "pro" at "crastination."

Every Thursday night around 10:30 p.m., I wait to hear those three pitiful words echo at me from upstairs, "Coulda, shoulda, woulda, Jane," my dad says in a tired tone. One would think after 16 years of "putting off for tomorrow what I could have gotten done today," my dad would realize that Ben Franklin was making an exception for me when he uttered those famous words. But alas, no.

Most teachers and parents don't realize this, but procrastination is indeed a talent. Not just anybody can finish homework ahead of time his whole life and suddenly switch to putting it off until the night before. It just doesn't work. Procrastination is like any other gene, you must be born with it.

Some might say the lucky ones are those who have not been blessed with the gift of time wasting. Sure, we "dilly dalliers" have late nights every now and then, often survived by energy drinks, loud music, coffee runs and alarm clocks to keep us from dozing off, but the life of a procrastinator does have its rewards.

In order to procrastinate successfully, one must be fully aware of when the assignment is due at least one to two weeks ahead of time. This way, you won't accidentally get a head start on that speech for Public Speaking and be, dare I say ... prepared? Ooh, I shudder at the mere thought.

Rule number two is very important, yet often confusing, so pay attention. No true procrastinator ever turns in the assignment after it's due. That is what we in the craft would call a "Diva Dawdler." There is a fine, yet distinct line between putting together a project at the last minute and turning it in late. The professional procrastinator has no missing assignments, nor has he used up any of his allotted "late" passes, no matter what the course of study.

Even classes like Outdoor Living or Cooking, where opportunities for putting things off are admittedly rare, present some prospects for delay tactics. For the wilderness folk, here's a couple fishing tips I perfected in the Boundary Waters. First, don't reel in your prize until everyone else has not only snagged, but boated his fish. Second, don't bait your hooks until it's time for "last call" casts. And for all the chefs out there, take some advice from an old pro and preheat the oven at 250 degrees versus everyone else's timely 350.

Well, I think it's time for me to head off to bed. But first, I think I'll grab a glass of water, brush my teeth, check my e-mail, maybe count some sheep....

Agendas Provide Road Map for Life

OCTOBER 20

- -

STANDING NEARLY 11 INCHES TALL AND A FULL 6 INCHES WIDE, THIS personal, plastic planner has it all. Complete with assignment calendar, events planner, world map, algebraic conversions, grammar tips, even the periodic table of elements, this small man-made wonder is every high-schooler's road map to success.

I received my first Agenda in fifth grade and was never more excited to copy down my list of nightly homework. I remember the two colorful designs that morphed into each other as I shifted the water-resistant cover back and forth in my hands. Opening the organizer, my eyes danced across the pages packed with information about seemingly every fact known to man.

For my next discovery, I was elated to excavate my ultra-cool, ultra-special gel pens out of the plastic pencil case hidden in my desk. Gel pens were a must-have at the time, and I saved mine for special occasions such as this. Toward the bottom of the first page of my Agenda, I cautiously printed both my name and "Silas Willard Elementary" on the dotted line. On the next page, there was an "All about Me" section where I wrote down my hobbies, favorite sports and goal-oriented questions about my dream college and occupation. Looks as if my assignment planner just turned into a life planner!

Eventually, I reached the main point of the Agenda, the weekly assignments/events calendar. From elementary school through junior high, each day of the calendar was divided into five sections: math, social studies, English, science and health. Most of the girls and I took organization to a whole other level by color-coding each subject. Boys, on the other hand, usually take the "au natural" approach and prefer to pencil in their dates and times.

Believe it or not, the decorating doesn't stop there! Besides being a beacon of time management, Agendas give my classmates and me another opportunity to show off our creativeness. Shellacked with stickers or garnished with glitter, a glamorous Agenda is often held up as a model for all the other envious notebooks that get toted from class to class. In addition, Agenda pages become storytellers as they are covered with photos of friends, classmates, family or even the family pet. After the Cardinals won the World Series last year, my Agenda became a frame for the overjoyed faces of Albert Pujols, Jim Edmonds and Scott Rolen.

Quotes of the week are found at the top of every page with words of wisdom to carry me on from Monday through Friday. This week's quote by Christopher Morley reads, "There is only one success - to be able to spend life in your own way."

Indeed, looking back through my now much-worn plastic pals from previous years, the road maps reveal proof positive that, so far anyway, I've traveled down my own chosen path.

Dyeing Your Hair? Read the Box Carefully

OCTOBER 27

- -

HALLOWEEN CAME EARLY THIS YEAR, LAST SATURDAY TO BE EXACT. Like most years, the tricks came before the treats.

All week long I had the urge to dye my hair. A healthy dose of the product Sun-In had been pushing me toward blonde for months and I wanted to get back to the real me. Coincidentally, one of my best friends, Emma, was planning on dyeing hers as well. With the highly unusual prospect of a Saturday free of commitments, I picked out the shade "soft black" from the back of the coloring box, hoping that it would counter the lighter highlights and return my hair to its authentic medium brown. After about an hour of shellacking the chemical goo all over my scalp, I hesitantly turned to the mirror. To my dismay, the "medium brown" I was shooting for didn't turn out so medium. With hair now blacker than licorice and darker than the night sky, I had become a witch in search of a broom to take flight. With the celebration of ghouls and goblins fast approaching, it looked as if my costume were already chosen for me.

Just as anyone else in my situation, the only interjection that came to mind was, "wow." Being such a loyal friend, Emma told me she loved the black and "wouldn't have it any other way." Not fully over the new 'do, I had to pull a double-take every time I passed a mirror. Was that me or the quirky sorceress from "Hocus Pocus?" It was after being mistaken for the wrong person at school Monday that I decided it was time to go back to my roots, literally.

A return trip to Walgreens to choose a lighter shade of coloring took half an hour, re-dyeing my hair took another hour, and getting over my reflection in the bathroom mirror after the second dyeing, well, I'm still struggling. It seems the word "permanent" on the bottom of the box is there for a reason. Perhaps it should be in a little bolder print. Feeling like I was caught up in a bad nightmare in which my hair was identical to the mane of Black Beauty, I became desperate for solutions. I almost tried a suggestion of washing my hair in dish soap, but thankfully, my hairstylist Tania came to a 7 p.m. rescue.

After several scoldings and good-natured beatings with the empty box of "soft black" dye, I received a gold star in what not to do with hair. Two hours later, I hesitantly looked in the vanity mirror of the salon. Thankfully, this time, the witch and her broomstick were gone.

Student council will once again host Haunted High School from 5 to 7 p.m. Monday at Galesburg High School. Thanks to miracle workers disguised as hairstylists and a pinch of patience, I can create my own costume from a consensus of what's in my cranium, not what's on top of it.

Jazzercise Jane Gets Gold Star for Sleeping

NOVEMBER 3

- -

UPON RECEIVING THE USUAL, DAILY QUESTION, "WHAT DID YOU LEARN in school today," I responded to my mom with a not so ordinary answer: "I learned how to sleep." I'm sure she took my response as sarcasm, which explains why she followed up with a surprised, "What?!"

Yes, it is true. Today's fourth-hour class was what we Individual Fitness students like to call "Relaxation Friday."

Because I am no longer participating in marching band, I needed a physical education class in my curriculum. So, this Monday was my first gym class experience at Galesburg High School. Let me just say, I wish I would have taken it sooner.

When I think aerobics, visions of lime green sweatbands, full-on, blown-out perms and hot pink leg warmers fill my memory. Thanks to my mom carting me around with her while she taught step aerobics in the early '90s, I will forever hear the voice of Richard Simmons when anyone uses the word "jazzercise."

To my relief, Coach Marla Clay got the class started off with some familiar beats, and before I knew it, I was doing the step aerobics I swore I would never bear witness to again. To my even greater disbelief, I was actually enjoying that blast from the past. Even the males in the room were catching the groove and participating in each move and step with non-disguisable grins on their faces.

After a few days of aerobics, walking around the track, and many crunches, my fellow classmates and I were "feeling the burn." Thursday was the last day of school this week, so Coach Clay treated it like a Friday. At the beginning of class, we walked for thirty minutes around the gym and then came my favorite part. I grabbed a gray mat from the shelves in the supply closet and found a spot to stretch out on the floor among my friends, Jorden, Bri, Rachel and Katie. A few seconds later, every light in John Thiel Gym was extinguished and the only sound to be heard came from the meditation video set up for us. Waterfalls, leaves, flowers and all sorts of nature scenes illuminated the screen. In the background, there was a voice of an instructor giving suggestions on how to relax. Ideas like pretending to be weightless and freeing the mind of all stress proved successful as ten minutes into the video, I was out like a light.

All in all, Individual Fitness is going to be a very helpful part of my school time as well as my day in general. Two things I thought I'd never see have already come to fruition in this new term, Jazzercise Jane and a gold star for dozing off in class.

It's a wonderful life indeed!

Where Would Bread Be Without Butter?

NOVEMBER 10

WHERE WOULD BATMAN BE WITHOUT ROBIN, LAVERNE MINUS HER Shirley, or Lewis stumbling across the wilderness without Clark? The same way peanut butter needs jelly, every student needs a "right hand man" or two.

Anyone who knows me wouldn't say I was the most graceful or flexible person walking the halls of GHS. However, I did not let my clumsiness bring me down when coming across a flyer earlier this week.

The canary yellow paper taped on one of the hallway doors called for a couple spots to be filled on the basketball cheerleading squads. Turning to my good pal Jorden, a veteran of the girls cheerleading squad for basketball, I made an offhand joke that went something like, "Wouldn't I make a great cheerleader?"

Much to my surprise, Jorden wasn't laughing. "Oh, you totally should!" she exclaimed with one of those "I've just had an idea" grins beaming across her face.

After the instant dismissal of Jorden's encouraging words, something inside me asked, "Well, why not?" Sure, I may be somewhat of a "Clutzy McClutz" every now and then, but if I was lucky enough to become a cheerleader, maybe I could learn how to fall a little less often, or at least go down with a smile on my face! Who knows? Maybe my odd ability to stumble rather than tumble could prove a positive trait. I mean, if I fell, at least I would be doing my job by forcing a round of applause from the crowd.

With the help of my two spectacular friends, Jorden and Alexa, all fears of forgetting the chant or shuffling out of step were thankfully cleared from blocking my confidence during try-outs. With the encouragement of these great pals and their efforts to show me the beginner's ropes at what they've been doing for years in a matter of two days, I am now a GHS girl's basketball cheerleader. In return for the support I received from my friends this past week, I hope to give back to the school by supporting the Streaks in each game by cheering them on to victory.

Next week is American Education Week and Student Council is showing our bountiful gratitude toward those hardworking men and women who get us to school, through school, and keep us coming back each day. Each student in District 205 has his or her own support team made up of the best bus drivers, sweetest secretaries and coolest custodians, as well as the most superb staff and talented teachers standing behind us through every step of our education.

On a daily basis, one, if not all, of these wonderful people at GHS may serve as our right-hand man. They show us the ropes by putting the cape on the crusader, offering Shirley-like advice or guiding us through the wilderness of high school. To all of you, thanks for spreading a little jelly on our peanut butter.

It's Hard to Connect in a Connected World

NOVEMBER 17

- -

"RRRRRING RRRRING!" GOES THE TELEPHONE. "BRRRRR BRRRRR," vibrates the text message on the cell phone. "You've got mail," says the computer. The background set has Mom with one ear tuned to the GHS football game on WGIL while Dad chuckles over his fiber-enriched bowl of Great Grains as, for the thousandth time, Kramer comes bursting into Seinfeld's apartment on the kitchen television screen.

With all these distractions, I often wonder how I meet any obligation, whether it be a homework assignment or a chore around the house. Of course, whenever I explain this dilemma to my parents, they always reach the same conclusion. Turn the phone on silent mode, back away from the TV, and turn the computer off altogether. Hmm, why didn't I think of that? Aparently, that lecture about the text-messaging charge on the last phone bill just hasn't quite gotten through to me.

Being a high school student in today's world is, in one adjective, busy. It seems like whenever I finish one activity, I'm rushing off to the next meeting, class or practice. Which reminds me, I think I'm going to ask Santa for a hardcore pair of running shoes for Christmas!

Given the craziness that comes along with being a teenager, it is important to us to feel connected with the outside world, a.k.a chat with our friends about the late-breaking news of the day. Enter cell phone, stage left. I never thought I'd see the day where someone could talk to her best friend, parents, and foreign exchange classmate from Australia all at the same time. Thanks to the addition of texting and "IM'ing," (that's Instant Messaging for you non-distracted folks) to cell phones worldwide, this ability to communicably multitask is no longer a dream or, as my Dad would say, nightmare. His idea of multitasking is a canoe paddle in one hand, a fishing pole in the other, and both ears full of silence.

It's true. Despite this newfound ability to converse with each other, there are some costly side effects. For instance, when trying to "solve for y" during an Algebra II equation, the tune "Yankee Doodle" blaring from someone's purse doesn't exactly make for a focused environment, especially if it's my purse. Thanks to similar incidents, we now have strict enforcement of the "No Cell Phone" policy at GHS.

My personal technological weakness is without a doubt, the computer. As a place of information and exploration of all things imaginable, the Gateway is easily my favorite resource for any American Studies presentation or just learning in general. Nevertheless, the computer is also my worst enemy when it comes to typing any form of paper. Before opening Microsoft Word, the first icon I click is the music player so I can listen to my favorite songs (in the background of course). Then it's a quick check of the ol' e-mail, a chat with a few of my friends on MSN, and hours later I'm ready to type.

In conclusion, I would have to say that distractions ... hang on a second, my pager's beeping me ...

Siblings Bust a Move

NOVEMBER 24

WITH THE COMING AND GOING OF ANOTHER SIMKINS THANKSGIVING, I find myself appreciating more than just family and friends. Specifically, my brother John and I exchange a gift that cannot be wrapped in a box, well maybe . . . if we're talking about a boom box!

Ever since mom displayed her love for getting down with moves such as "the grapevine" and "the pony," my brother and I have been updating the Simkins dance-move arsenal. With the beat in our feet and our shoes in the groove, we have taken the family "electric slide" to a whole new stratus.

Some of our moves were inspired by music videos or the ever-popular MTV. Growing up in the '90s, artists like Will Smith, Run DMC and the Beastie Boys were, literally, a big influence on our every move. Anyone who's ever been a fan of "The Fresh Prince of Bel-Air" remembers the episode where Carlton and Will perform the infamous "Apache" routine. For those who have never experienced that scene, I suggest you check it out on YouTube, pronto. Recently, with the advances in musical technology, John and I often send each other new songs we discover, for the other one's approval of whether it's "off the hook" or just off.

Living without our own personal dance floor seemed a drag at first, but we took advantage of our resources enough to get us through the '90s. I believe cardboard was involved. . .

Anywho, once dad the handyman installed wood floors in all the rooms of the house, he should have just cranked the tunes right then and there! John and I finally got to wave farewell to rug burn and were forever sanctioned from the wrath of mom for "marking up the carpet."

Perhaps the best addition to all our rooms were track lights that run across our ceiling like mini spotlights just asking for a dance party. The lighting of the first bulb established the Simkins Dance Party of 2000, and even though they've been ejected from the house, we're still "cuttin' a rug."

Tonight, I reflect on my many blessings of recent history. My grandma Mary Sue is healing from her surgery and will hopefully break out of the hospital tomorrow. I was also witness to the relief and joy of Mom and Dad seeing my college dance partner make his usual "I'm home, let the party begin" entrance into the kitchen safe and sound. This celebration, at the end of seven hours of sliding and sloshing the Monte Carlo from St. Paul to Galesburg, commences each Thanksgiving Eve with our dog Boomer slopping wild kisses upon the face of the favorite son.

The annual catching up with cousins from Iowa and within the 'Burg fills our kitchen with the echoes of laughter and storytelling. Grandparents, aunts and uncles, and the occasional new addition to the family like cousin Brence, keep the old stories fresh and the new ones ready for next year's editing. This Thanksgiving I'd like to give a shout out to my family, for putting the "jive" in my "jive turkey" since 1991.

I hope all of you were able to cut a little rug or, if not, some Thanksgiving bird with family and friends this year. Perhaps, what I'm most thankful for is the four-day break from sitting in class. I'll need it to Chubby Checker away that pumpkin pie and sweet potatoes. Hey, John, where's the boom box and cardboard?

Lack of Wheels Leaves Time to Think

DECEMBER 1

- -

I WAS FIVE YEARS OLD STANDING OUTSIDE OF SILAS WILLARD Elementary School searching for my grandma's black car like a needle in a moving haystack. My mom was going to be working late and my dad wouldn't be home from the fire station until the next day, so I was told to look for my grandma's car after school. I looked, but no car. Standing at the bottom of the steps I felt like a rock in a river of salmon while all the other kids glided past me and into their mini vans. "Could she have forgotten?" I inquired towards myself. "No, no, never...well, maybe..., no, she wouldn't, would she?"

I gripped my Aladdin backpack for dear life when, fifteen minutes later, the little black sedan and my grandma were still M.I.A. as well as the rest of my classmates and their rides. If not for the gracious act of my kindergarten teacher Mrs. Renfroe to call my grandma, I might still be standing on those steps.

This past Thursday, I stood gazing through the fingerprint-covered door on the west end of GHS, waiting for the family Buick to pull into the school parking lot. Despite searching car lots and hearing promises from over-cautious parents, I remain a junior without wheels. After about fifteen minutes, I remembered the words of my mom, "You'll have to ask a friend for a ride home today." Immediately, that anxious feeling of being left behind swept over me as I scanned the bare parking lot for any glimpse of hope. I felt like I was five again. A five-year-old with a cell phone that is.

One phone call to my dad later, I decided to make the most of my time until he came to pick me up. Unzipping my book bag, I dragged out my American Studies book and got to work on some key terms. Out of all the places I have ever studied, the loudest wing of the school, the music hallway, ended up being the perfect studying environment. Practicing two doors down was the Jazz Band, and let me tell you, I would choose their awesome sound over any of my CD's!

For maybe the first time I was actually "in" the hallway, not just zipping through it to another destination. I got to appreciate decorations such as posters promoting various clubs and handmade locker signs for the athletic teams. I even noticed that the tile in the band hallway is shaped to look like musical notes on a staff. Now that's what I call creative! Surrounded by all that classy jazz music from my old band buddies and eye-catching décor designed by my classmates and teammates, I no longer felt like a nervous kindergartner. I felt like a confident sixteen-year old. I felt...at home.

Shortly after, Dad's old pickup came rumbling around the corner, oblivious to the speed bumps, and pulled up, slinging the passenger door open. Jumping in, the lecture began – "you know, you could always walk – in my day, I used to have to……." And to think those salmon really want to return home each year.

American Studies Shows History Where It's At

DECEMBER 8

THEY CALL ME BOW, CLARA BOW.

The "Roaring Twenties" is the time period we've been recently learning about in American Studies class. One of my favorite aspects of American Studies is the informational, yet exciting learning atmosphere it provides.

Eye rolls and the sarcastic "Yeah right" are the reactions of friends when I rave about how pumped I am to get to American Studies class. For those that still say there's no way history can be fun, let me share this awesome assignment and state my case.

Last week, my classmates and I were each given a famous character from the 1920s to research. These ranged from Babe Ruth, the "Great Bambino," to Charlie Chaplin, the "Little Clown." After getting a clearer image of our icon, we were told that we'd be taking a walk in their shoes … literally. This Friday, my classmates and I are dressing up in full costume and stirring around the classroom in full character, walking and talking in the shoes of our assigned celebrity.

When Mrs. Aten first matched my name with that of Clara Bow, I was completely in the dark. I soon discovered through clips of some silent films from the '20s and excerpts from various library books that I would be portraying the first "It" girl known to America.

Bow had everything a woman of that era secretly envied: the bee-stung lips, beautifully made-up face, a spunky bob, and the confidence of a lion-tamer. Reading about this woman who had "It" provided me with a sense of her, on and off the big screen. However, what I thought would be a simple task turned out to require a lot more effort.

First off, I had to perfect the Brooklyn accent, keeping it a little more "Laverne" than "Shirley." After a little bit of brushing up on the speech department, I moved on to the famous spitfire Bow personality. Clara was not one to be subtle, demonstrated by her opinion of the less-fair sex, "The more I see of men, the more I like dogs."

Next, I needed to nail down the most essential element of the character, the wardrobe. When most people think of Clara Bow, one word comes to mind - flapper. In many of her movie roles, Bow was a flirty, flapper-like girl wearing high heels, shorter skirts, heavy eye makeup and enough costume jewelry to fill Lake Michigan. Thus, my outfit: black mini dress, metallic gold pumps, black headband with gold designs, umpteen fake-pearl necklaces with gold chains, and eye makeup so intense as to make even Cleopatra's lashes look downplayed.

My classmates are getting into their characters as well. Take my friend Daniel. He's slicking back his dark wavy locks and donning enough suaveness to put the real Rudolph Valentino to shame. My friend Olivia's going so far as to sport her swim team suit with some sweats to resemble the famous female swimmer, Esther Williams.

American Studies gives everyone, including non-history buffs, a chance to step outside the textbook and physically grasp the flavor of every decade in America's past.

Still think history is boring and tedious? I'm hanging with the old Mae West line, "Too much of a good thing is wonderful."

Pssst, Jane's Up to Your Challenge

DECEMBER 15

- -

"PSSST, DON'T LET JANE BE A BASE, THERE'S NO WAY SHE'S STRONG enough to put anyone up, let alone catch them." - Anonymous Cheerleader

"Pssst, Tom, don't let Jane drive the Buick on the ice, there's no way she's got the skills to handle those slick roads." - Marcy Simkins a.k.a. my mom

"Pssst, Doc Joe, give Jane some more numbing medicine, there's no way she'll manage the pain from the drill." - Assistant to the Orthodontist

From the looks of those comments, it's painfully obvious that some people had little faith in my abilities this week. At this point I could have, A.) Thrown in the towel and taken a back seat in my own life, or B.) Turned each one of those skeptics into believers by taking on their doubts as challenges. I'm proud to say I decided to roll with Option B on this one. However, the whole "roll" part turned out to be more of a "rock."

At cheerleading practice on Monday, I took the opportunity of joining a stunt group that had been missing their second base. Hands shaking, mind racing, I asked for a little bit of instruction on how exactly I was to lift a human being above my head, with a smile on my face. Expecting a "hands on" demonstration, Sharpie-drawn illustration, or verbal breakdown, I was shocked when all I got was, "just don't drop her." Backing out was almost my plan of action until those words, "no way she's strong enough" racked my mind, and before I knew it, in two counts I instantaneously became a base. I think that was the only time I've seen a cheerleader at a loss for words!

As far as driving on the ice, both the Buick and the Jane made it back in one piece after I cautiously drove to indoor soccer practice during the remnants of the big ice storm Tuesday night. Thankfully, the only thing that got shredded that night were my doubters! Not only did I gain more experience as a driver, I think my parents have a newfound confidence in my skills. Is that a car I see in my future?

With basing and improved driving skills under my belt, I only had one more issue to tackle, and this time I added a personal dash of fear to the equation. A common villain named Mr. Shot was my arch nemesis Thursday when I paid a visit to my orthodontist, Doctor Joe. Not only did I endure and overcome the numbing sting of three shots, I went on to cheer my lungs out at the Varsity Girls basketball game that same night with half my face tied behind my back. A few crooked-lipped smiles, and laughs later, I was back in action basing and driving in icy conditions.

"Pssst, don't ever let Jane cheer with a Novocained mouth again; we kept wondering why she was cheering for the Sweaks" - The Student Section

Christmas Tradition with a Twist

DECEMBER 22

- -

I DECIDED TO TAKE A NEW SPIN ON THE TRADITIONAL CHRISTMAS story this year, and it goes a little something like this ...

'Twas the night before Christmas Break and all through the school, not a teacher was scolding, not a student breaking a rule.

My gym clothes were folded in my locker with pride, begging for someone to wash them with Tide.

During Relaxation, I drifted off as coach Clay read, while visions of Winter Break sleep-ins danced in my head.

After Advisory there arose such a clatter, I sprang from my desk smelling Christmas cookie batter.

Away to the lunchroom I made a mad dash, ate my garden salad and tossed all my trash.

The sunlight beamed from the new fallen snow and reflected through Mr. Allison's biology window.

When, what on the chalkboard to my eyes should appear, but the word DISSECTION, oh how my heart pounded with fear.

More rapid than reindeer, second block came. What? No home-work? Oh, what a ... shame!

The time ticked away to the end of the day, I could no longer wait for wintertime play.

Now sledding, now snowballs, now hot chocolate mugs, on carols, on tree lights, on Santa Claus!

And then, in a twinkling, I heard in the hall, holiday music for one and for all.

As I walked down the steps, what came to my sight, but a beautifully drawn menorah all dressed up with light.

The Christmas Tree, too, was decked out to a "T," thanks to student council's decorating committee.

The holiday spirit in my classmates no doubt, I could hear in each whisper and behind every shout.

Before I knew it, Friday was done and I was ready for Christmastime fun.

So fling back the doors and dig out your stash - where's mom and the Buick? - to the mall with some cash!

Bring on the presents, the laughter, the cousins, and cook up the ham and the rolls by the dozens.

But mostly remember at this time of year, to pass with the rolls a pint of good cheer.

Happy Holidays and Merry Christmas, everyone, from my journal to yours.

Four-Wheeled Black Beauty is Her Red Ryder

DECEMBER 29

- -

I'M NOT ONE FOR SURPRISES, MAINLY BECAUSE I USUALLY END UP unveiling the surprise before I'm supposed to. The worst part is trying to pretend to be in shock and exclaiming with watered down excitement "I had no idea!" When really, I knew exactly what was going to happen all along.

This Christmas however, I was completely blindsided when my parents presented me with the one gift almost every teenager dreams about, one that won't fit in any box and would be nearly impossible to wrap.

The whole scheme started off with a video camera in my face when I came down the steps Christmas morning. I'm not exactly what most would call a morning person and the last thing I wanted was someone getting evidence of that fact on tape. But after a few pleas to "please get the camera out of my face," I finally gave up.

Being the youngest (and shortest) in the family it was my job to remove all the presents out from under the tree and pass them out to everyone. A couple pair of dangly earrings and some clothing items later, I began tossing away the now wrinkled wrapping paper scattered throughout the living room. I still clung to a slight hope that maybe, just maybe, I would somehow discover a hint of a 4-wheeled version of Ralphie's Red Ryder under that tree or behind the couch, and all would be right with the world. But alas, no sign of a vehicle of my own from "Santa" was to be found. Luckily, my hopes had not been set too high, so I really wasn't all that bummed when no car appeared.

As I sat down on the couch next to my dad, I noticed he had the video camera directed right at me. Turning to ask him once again to "put the camera away" I noticed this time he was holding something in his hands. Could it be? No way? Wait, it is! A sly grin emerged under his mustache as, with video camera still in hand, he said "Merry Christmas Jane."

There, dancing mid-air in all its glory was a key with the Honda symbol inscribed on top. I, Jane Simkins, was the proud owner of a 1996 Honda Accord, and for the first time in my life, I was honestly surprised.

Racing out to the garage, brother trailing behind me, I threw open the snowy door to find a black beauty awaiting me. Even with my dad still videotaping, the sound of the engine starting up as I turned the key for the first time drowned out all other distractions.

And so it was this Christmas, that I indeed became Ralphie; not by clinging to a Red Ryder and dreaming of pranging birds on the wing with fantastic hip shots, but sitting in my Black Pearl listening to the CD player while dream-cruising down Fremont Street. Even with the increased parental warnings of "Go slow, those bricks streets are icy" replacing Ralphie's "you'll shoot your eye out kid," I could think of only one word . . . FREEDOM!

Forget the Future, Get on with the Past

JANUARY 5

- -

I'M NOT MUCH OF A HISTORY BUFF, BUT THESE PAST COUPLE OF weeks, I've been getting in touch with something that most people, let alone teenagers, rarely discover ... my past.

The quest in digging to my roots was inspired by an assignment to reflect upon what I learned from studying the 1920s and 30s era this past term. The blank Word document that lay before me waited impatiently to file away everything I knew about the Great Depression, the Dust Bowl and F.D.R.'s New Deal. However, what became of this one assignment turned into more than a generic paragraph listing facts uncovered from my American Studies book.

I was bitten by a bug. The history bug that is. How can I tell? Well, for the first time in a while, I focused on, and thoroughly enjoyed, an in-class movie. It's probably not fair to compare an Oscar-winning film to an outdated, low-budget, "Safety in the Bio Lab" instructional tape, but "Cinderella Man" was the best movie I've ever witnessed while seated in a classroom.

For those that have yet to see the movie, I won't give away too many details, except that it is set in the late 1920s to the mid-'30s and tells the story of one young family trying to scrape up enough money to pay the bills and put food on the table. The power behind this video gave me the drive to better understand this time in our history and, believe it or not, to read my history book with enthusiasm!

Currently, I am over halfway finished with my other assignment, "The Grapes of Wrath," a classic novel written by John Steinbeck about a family who moves west during the Depression in hopes of a better life. Reading isn't necessarily one of my favorite pastimes either, but with a better connection to the era, I uncharacteristically find myself having to be told to put the book down and get some sleep.

The best part about this whole "getting in touch with my past" deal is the way I've brought this interest in history to my everyday life here in the 21st Century. Thursday for instance, I traveled to Abingdon to visit my Grandma Shirley and the first things I noticed on her bookshelf were her 1940's yearbooks. Astounded to think that my grandparents actually lived through everything I had been learning about these past few weeks, I began hunting for more photos and recollections from the 1930s. Amazingly, in a time with little technology, no cell phones, stereos, or iPods, what stood out in the old photos were the genuine smiles and something that might be called "togetherness" of the era. Once again, I had to be pried away from reading.

All this researching makes me wonder about the day my grandchildren will tear through the pages of my GHS yearbooks. I'm sure after a good talking to for making fun of how Grandma Jane wore her hair back in the day, I'll tell them stories about my life growing up in the "tens." I guess it's like the old saying goes, "you can't have a future, without first learning from your past." Thanks, Grandma, for showing me a little of our "Cinderella" story.

O, Brother, Where Art Thou?

JANUARY 12

- -

MY BROTHER AND I WENT TO SCHOOL TOGETHER FOR ONE YEAR. WE attended Silas Willard Elementary. I was 5 and he was 10. I had a big gap in my teeth, his was between his ears. We shared one class with each other everyday, recess, which granted me the opportunity of perpetually pestering him for 15 minutes. Yelling "John's a big doofus" during his pick-up game of basketball, was a moment I cherished each and everyday. On the other hand, I didn't look forward to the 6-block walk home every afternoon with him trailing behind me, chucking buckeyes at the back of my head as his form of revenge. I think that's where he honed his pitching skills that served him in later years.

Fortunately, my first-grade year found John stepping up on the ladder of education and maturity when he traded in his "Transformers" backpack for the oh-so-cool, Nike book bag and headed off to Churchill

Junior High. The change was gradual, but eventually John became more involved in school, especially with athletics like baseball and soccer. Fortunately, my head was spared from further loss of brain cells by giant acorns, but I quickly realized that I missed my "recess ridicule ritual," and seeing my brother in general.

It took a few weeks to learn how to peacefully walk home in a straight line rather than following my usual zigzag pattern for dodging buckeyes. However, I eventually graduated to Churchill myself, and now I'm finally in sight of my last year of high school, brother-free and independent. Well, at least that's what I thought until my older sibling began aiding classes at GHS during his winter break from Macalester College in St. Paul, Minn.

Never did I think we'd be walking down the same hallways and eating the same lunch ever again. As a matter of fact, the first time I passed John in the hallway it didn't hit me that he was my brother turned teacher. Not until he rode with me to school Tuesday in the Black Pearl did I realize that the old days were back, minus the whole "hurling bits of nature at Jane" part, of course. Also shocking was that I finally put a cap on the "ridiculing John" bottle, which was especially difficult since we shared the same gym in P.E. three days this week.

Weird but comforting is how I would describe reliving the past this week with my brother. Weird in the sense that I felt like I was on an episode of "The Twilight Zone" struck with a bad case of deja-vu. Comforting in the sense that even as I unconsciously walked the halls of GHS in serpentine fashion this week, there were two eyes facing forward and a smile on my face. It seems that as we have grown apart, we have also grown together. With the 5-year span between us now seeming smaller and the normal 400-mile distance between us down to 4 dribbles of the basketball, the "doofus" now seems more brother than bother.

Path from Observer to Participant Difficult

JANUARY 19

- -

EVER HAVE ONE OF THOSE WEEKS WHERE NOTHING SEEMS TO GO right? For this high schooler, the past five-day stretch has been one of those type weeks.

Where do I begin? Ah yes, let's start off with my quasi-black eye. Performing a "cradle-down" from our cheerleading stunt, our flyer came down as my good friend (and back spot) Caitlin's fist accidentally came up and into my left eye. Of course, Caitlin felt bad and apologized for the accident. However, the tables quickly turned as I pulled a Rocky Balboa on Caitlin's lower jaw with my own fist during another stunt. This time I was on the other side of the fence, apologizing to her. It was only Tuesday and I had almost managed to wipe out a fellow stunt groupie and myself. What a way to start off the week, eh? Oh, well, I saved a little mascara on that left eye.

Before I forget, let me trace back to Monday when all my shabby shenanigans began. Monday marked the beginning of second semester at GHS and my normal routine was traded for a new class schedule. One would think that after two and a half years of attending the high school I would've known the exact location of any class my counselor threw at me. Well, my friends, think again.

Standing outside the door marked with my teacher's name plate, it didn't occur to me to read the sign stating, "Mr. Benewitz, Journalism 1 - Room 208 (an upstairs classroom)." Aimlessly, I stood in front of the door downstairs peering into the empty room waiting for my new teacher to arrive. If it weren't for the help of another teacher, I would still be waiting by the wrong door. So, I was late for my first day of fourth hour. Awesome first impression, huh?

When I'm not handing out knuckle sandwiches to my best buddies or walking into class late, I'm receiving my first ticket. And I'm not talking about concerts or movies. Yes, I'll admit it I, Jane Simkins, received a citation for not wearing my seat belt Wednesday during my usual trek to school. Probably one of the most embarrassing times of my life, seeing those lights flashing in my rear-view mirror had me shaking like John Travolta in "Saturday Night Fever." Although I looked like a skittish 5-year-old calling her dad for help, I realized the time had come for me to reap the consequences of my own actions. I couldn't just sit in the back seat and laugh while my dad received the ticket, like I had at the ripe old age of 7. No, this time it was all on me. I had no one to look at but myself. That and the couple hundred students who drove by gawking as the police officer wrote me up, and did I say, right in front of the high school.

I understand now I'm no longer the passenger in the backseat of my life. It's my turn to take the wheel and learn how to get back on the road when I hit a bump. And when all else fails, well, at least I've got a left eye to match my car.

Jammed Gym Brilliant in Blackout

JANUARY 26

THE NIGHT WAS DARK. NO, SCRATCH THAT. THE NIGHT WAS BLACK. Yeah, really black. So black you could say the night was "blacked-out." That's right. But the night turned especially dark for the raucous Pioneers faithful who happened to wander out of a well-lit parking lot and into John Thiel Gym on Thursday night as the Silver Streaks fab five and their fans lit things up for "Jam the Gym Night."

In support of the well-advertised "Blackout" theme, nearly every Silver Streak performing on the floor as well as in the crowd was decked out in black. With the team running like a well-oiled machine, there was plenty of envy in the green uniforms on the backs of the Pioneers. But there are also a lot of well-deserved shout-outs I would like to administer toward certain groups of students for cheering our beloved Streaks on to victory, starting with the biggest group of all, the student section.

There's nothing like the roar of a huge crowd to get the team pumped for a big conference game like the GHS girls versus Rock Island Alleman. Thanks to my fellow classmates, none of our baskets went un-appreciated and no time out went silent. For the cheerleaders, it's always a great feeling to get our Streaks in the bleachers riled up and chanting with us. Though there are over 50 of us shaking pompoms on the floor, we appreciate guys like Jordan, Sean, Brian, Tanner and Rogue helping us get everyone involved. When one of our players got knocked around a little too much, the GHS student section healed her wounds with some encouraging shouts ... and a little help from the first aid kit (thanks Coach P.)

What good would any ball game be without some marvelous musicians to get the feet tapping and the spirits up? Our cheerful pep band rocked the night at every break in the action and the talented choir vocalists got us off on the right foot while Senior Tom Fornander pulled the Stars and Stripes to the gym ceiling. I'm very gracious toward the band for the sweet song choices. "Hey, Baby" is always a classic pep song and you guys had nearly every person in that gym blasting the lyrics right with you. I'll take the GHS chamber choir's rendition over N'Sync's "Star Spangled Banner" any day. Oh, and before I forget, nice job on the solo, C.J.

For this year's Super Bowl, I nominate the GHS Gadets, Winter Guard and Drum Line to perform during the halftime show. Thursday night, the Gadets got groovy with a sort of "dancing through the decades" routine that gave me the urge to bust a move myself. During halftime of the sophomore game, the GHS Winter Guard amazed the crowd with their insanely exceptional flag and rifle routine. Each time one of the Guard members tosses a rifle high into the air, you can sense the entire gym holding its breath, only to exhale when it is skillfully snagged in mid-air. In keeping with the "Blackout" theme, there's no doubt the GHS Drum Line wears their sunglasses at night. And rightfully so, considering the brilliance they disperse any time they perform. The Drum Line always leaves the crowd wanting an encore, which they surprisingly got on Thursday. Thanks "Drum" for never leaving us hanging.

Despite the below zero temperatures and a blackout on Fremont Street Thursday, the gym was definitely jammin' as much as it was jammed.

Just Ask for Help and All Will be OK

FEBRUARY 2

LAST FRIDAY'S ALGEBRA QUIZ CAUGHT ME OFF GUARD LIKE A DEER IN the headlights. Although math has always been my weakest subject, I've never had trouble keeping up a good grade in any of my classes. So, when my teacher passed back my quiz and I saw that gloomy grade glaring back at me, my confidence level deflated quicker than a pin-popped birthday balloon. High scores are usually good, except of course when the grading scale is based on the alphabet. Unfortunately, in this case my exam grade was several letters down in the alphabet. As if the low grade wasn't enough, my score was written in the infamous and impossible to hide red pen. Nothing says, "you are incorrect" like good ol' red ink.

It was at this point in class that I was sucker-punched by a bolt from the blue. Shameful test in hand, I nearly broke rule numero uno of "the tough girl" policy ... crying in class. I'm not sure whether it was the lack of sleep from the previous night, or the home economics class chopping onions on the lower level of the building, but my eyes began to tear up. What do I do now? Am I the only one who didn't understand the material? Will this crush any hope of going to a good college? And that's when my eyes locked upon the daily quote written on the chalkboard, "Everything turns out okay in the end; if it's not okay, then it's not the end."

Whoa! Fireworks illuminated the classroom right then and there. I'm surprised I didn't see any pigs flying by the window. The answer to every question boggling my mind, the prescription for my loss of hope was scrolled out in soft white chalk. It wasn't the end of the world after all. The mid-term remains a week or so away, I'd still have a shot at pulling my grade up to satisfactory standards.

Now is the time for me to kick my studying into high gear and do whatever I need to gain confidence back in my mathematical skills. My math whiz friend Alexa met with me before cheer practice to help me see the light. My dad came to the rescue on Wednesday night and brightened the light bulb above my head with his old school brand of teaching.

I will continue to ask questions when I don't understand and refuse to feel ashamed or apologize if my inquiries appear "dumb."

Beginning this Super Bowl Sunday afternoon, you can find me at the Knox College Library, where a college student will make a few bucks boosting my math confidence for the week ahead.

Like anything in life, I am finding it is OK to ask for help, and starting next week, math will no longer be my weakest anything.

All Dressed Up and No Place to Go

FEBRUARY 9

FANCY DRESS? CHECK. SPARKLY SHOES? CHECK. "WOW, IS THAT really my hair" appointment? Check again. Hmmm ... Seems like something is missing. Aha! A date!

There'll be no "sweetheart" to my Swirl this year. Somewhere between the cheerleading practices, anticipation of the ACT exam and committee meetings, I lost track of time in asking a guy to the dance. OK, and maybe it was just too nerve- racking. After talking with my good friends Alexa, Maria, Monica and Jessie, it was clear we were all paddling solo in the same boat, all dressed up without a date. After about two minutes of brainstorming, we all came to the same conclusion, Project "D Cubed" (Dresses, Dinner and DVDs).

Of course, I'll miss the usual hullabaloo before the dance. Things like watching the guys flinch as their moms try pinning on their boutonnieres and the awkward posing in front of the dance theme backdrop. I will probably feel most left out about seeing all my classmates dressed up and showing off their version of the "coffee grinder" or the "electric slide" on the gym floor.

Not only will I be missing the dance; this will also be the first year I've missed out on decorating with student council the morning of Swirl. Instead, I'll be strapping on my thinking cap as I take on the "big poppa" of all tests, the ACT. Rather than hanging up streamers and tying balloons,

I will be solving chemistry equations and wearing out the leads of more than one No. 2 pencil. There's nothing like a good binary fission equation to wake you up in the morning!

Even though I won't be grooving under a disco ball, there's no stopping me from having a blast with my best pals on Saturday night. More than likely, I won't be missing out on all the dancing, considering whenever my comrades and I get together, none of us can stop from busting a goofy move or two. As far as a fancy out-of-town dinner goes, I'm pretty sure I'll be found dining out with my fellow femme fatales in one of the many grand restaurants on beautiful Seminary Street. Nothing beats a good, old-fashioned, home-cooked meal in the 'Burg.

Maybe next year I'll be more on the ball, and not wait until it's too late to track down a date. But for this year, Project "D Cubed" sounds good to me. The Swirl theme is "Under the New York Lights," although, in my case, I believe the lamps of Galesburg will suit my buds and me just fine!

Ode to Boomerang and Unconditional Love

FEBRUARY 16

YOU ARE THE LAST ONE TO SMILE AT ME EACH MORNING ON MY WAY to school. From your chair in the front window, you watch over my hurried exit down the driveway in the Black Pearl. As I step into the car some sixteen hours and a sad bus trip from Geneseo later, your smile is there to bring me back home. Maybe we lost the big game. Maybe I didn't get straight A's on my report card. Maybe I forgot to take you on that walk I promised yesterday. No matter how many times I messed up, lost, or forgot, you never judged me, but instead welcomed me with an excited, loving grin.

This is an ode to my dog. Yes, that's right, my smelly, slobbery, yippy, favorite-shoe-chewing dog, Boomerang.

We named you so because when we discovered you were an Australian Shepherd, well, "Dingo" and "Kangaroo" were already taken.

Of your various colored brothers and sisters, you came to us as the smallest, weakest pup of the litter. You were the runt. But even though you were the most petite in your family, you have proven to be the most loyal pet I've ever met. Unlike Shakespeare, the guinea pig, you did not make a break for it under the deck when I let you roam in the backyard. You quickly became my pal when John went away to college and you never hurled buckeyes at me. You truly are the best friend any man or 16-year old girl could ever hope for.

Even when I forgot your birthday four years in a row, you never reminded me of my ignorance or yelled at me for being "inconsiderate." Oh, and let's not forget about the time I accidentally pushed you off the back of the chair and you almost hurt your leg. I know I would have pushed me back! But you refrained from getting revenge because 1.) You don't have opposable thumbs, and 2.) You've got that amazing gift called unconditional love.

When no one else will play soccer with me, you're always there on all fours to block my advance, attacking the ball like a sheep gone astray. If not for you, I would never have become a midfielder. When it came to golf, you were probably more of a distraction, especially when you punctured all the practice balls. However, by the same token, you did help me to focus on my aim a little better!

You did so much for me I think it's time I started returning the favor. The next time I promise to take you for a walk around the block, I'll turn the block into a mile. The next time I promise to let you sleep on my bed, I won't put you back in your cage when you start to snore. And the next time someone asks me about my best friend, I'll remind myself of your loyalty and companionship. Boomerang, because even when I toss you off to the side like last week's stale bagel, you never fail to come right back to me.

Smile, You're on Simkins' Camera

FEBRUARY 23

I CAN PLAY A ROUND OF GOLF WITH MICHELLE WIE WITHOUT PRAC-ticing my swing every day. I can climb Mount Everest without ever taking a foot outside the classroom. I can even ride a T-rex without constructing a time machine. All it takes is a dose of imagination and a sprinkle of magic from Photoshop and I'm off into dreamland on a spectacular adventure.

Journalism class has expanded my thinking beyond pen and paper; it has opened the gates to a flood of creativity, digital creativity that is. Monday afternoon, Mr. Bennewitz announced to the class that we would be embarking on a new aspect of journalism, photography. But it wasn't until we watched a film on the rules of taking a professional, eye-catching picture that it hit me. My days of the "say cheese" and snap routine were long gone. If multi-media production was anywhere in my future career path, it was essential that I learn to produce well-organized snapshots. No more cutting off my best friend's head on every birthday picture. Goodbye red eye. Bye bye blurs. Adios background trees that appear to be growing out of my dad's head in the vacation albums. And no more will that black turtleneck make Mom's head appear detached and floating among us in the family picture. Henceforth, new and improved, well-balanced photographs are all that will come from this photographer's lens!

After a positive reflection on our photo taking skills, my classmate Zak and I were given the digital camera. We were assigned to take three photos of each other using the rules of photography we learned earlier in the week. Most of our film turned out with profile shots, looking up and slightly to the left. Why we looked to the left I have no idea, but it sure sounded like something the pros would do! My personal favorites were the action shots; however, I don't believe I'll be seeing them in Sports Illustrated any time soon.

Next on the to-do list was to edit our pictures using the sweet Photoshop program. This is where the project really became interesting. Using tools such as the "invisible wand," I could give myself a new hair-do or use the "lasso" tool to exchange my golf club for a light saber. Perhaps, the most impressive gadget is the "fill" which allowed me to transform my simple portrait into a stained-glass work of art in a matter of seconds.

This week I've received a new appreciation for every picture inserted into a magazine or newspaper. It does make one wonder, though, where does that perfect hairdo, extra lift in the biceps, or acne-free face find its roots in reality. Is it good genetics, is it the hairdresser or make-up person, or is it hours at the gym? Perhaps, only the "photoshopper" knows for sure.

'LUUUCEEE!'

MARCH 1

- -

LAUGHTER IS MY BEST ACCESSORY. LAUGHTER IS THE ATTENTION-GET-ter that can upscale a drab look from last year's worn-out trends into tomorrow's front-page Vogue. Laughter is my safety net that allows me to make fun of myself whenever I mess up. Laughter is the one language that does not need to be translated. Laughter is universal.

Making people laugh is my most adored hobby. Being able to paint a smile on someone's blank canvas brings me more joy than any shopping spree or test grade could ever provide. If I could achieve one dream, I would be cast in the starring role of a drop-dead comedy, leaving theater-goers of all ages and backgrounds rolling in the aisles.

In a way, my dream came true this past week in American Studies when I was presented with the role of the unbelievably funny Lucille Ball for a research project. In this activity, my classmates and I will be researching and acting the parts of various icons from the 1950s. We will present our characters together in a sort of "town meeting" fashion. Like Lucy's fiery red hair lighting up the screen, stepping into the character of this timeless comedian throws a dash of color into the bleakness of this long winter.

Although I'm sure some old "I Love Lucy" lines will ignite a few chuckles, there's no doubt my friends will get a kick out of my attempt at a Lucille Ball costume. Red hair, candy apple red lipstick, and the classic collection of Lucy's goofy facial expressions will be sure to bust a few guts. However, considering my "Hair Coloring Catastrophe of 2007," I'll have to settle for a red wig.

A few of my other classmates will flash back in fun roles as well. My friend Peter will star as a TV ad salesman, while Emily spins records as a radio DJ. Something tells me my buddy Olivia's representation of the "wealthy socialite" will tweak a few funny bones as well.

In order to get more in touch with my "Lucy" side, I plan on watch-ing a few of my favorite "I Love Lucy" episodes. The "Vitameatavegemin" episode has already helped me establish a repertoire of just a few of the many hilarious, contorted expressions of Lucy.

Of course, if all else fails to make me become the best Lucille Ball that I can be, who better to go to for advice than the funny lady herself. "Use a make-up table with everything close at hand and don't rush; otherwise you'll look like a patchwork quilt."

Grass Stains and Muddy Cleats are Back

MARCH 8

IMPRESSIVE GRASS STAINS ON SWEATY SHIN GUARDS AND MUD-caked cleats resembling mukluks can mean only one thing - spring soccer season has sprung!

But with Mother Nature and a few dozen eager participants impatiently waiting for Father Time to put enough calendar between us and a near-sighted groundhog, we are stuck with a thermometer reading reflecting my ACT score. Monday, March 3, my pompoms were replaced with gloves as we were forced to move our first official practice inside. Packing 30 players in one half of Wicall Gym wasn't exactly the easiest or best smelling task in the world. However, I was really surprised at how we were able to make do with the space we were given and ended up getting in some quality practice time. Slightly warmer weather eventually came our way as the week progressed, (42 degrees woo-hoo!) allowing us to be reacquainted with our beloved practice field.

It is common knowledge among most of the upperclassmen that the first couple of weeks into the season tend to be the most grueling. Partly, because it's tough to jolt our bodies out of winter hibernation mode and wake up those muscles we keep in storage for soccer season only. That would be those with the fast-twitch fibers capable of contorting in all sorts of directions granted to the chosen few, we soccer players.

The first few practices can be especially rough for the freshmen. Watching the expressions on some of their faces after the first practice reminded me of how I felt when I was in their cleats. One of the most significant memories I have is crawling up the stairs after practice, aching in places I never knew existed.

I also recall looking up to the juniors and seniors as if they were ESPN superstars. Noting every technique and skill they had mastered, I tried my best to keep up. Though I could hardly hold a candle to Mia Hamm or the GHS role models I once tried to imitate, it is because of them that I've decreased my "whiffing the ball" average by about 90 percent. More often than not, I now have some control of the ball, rather than it just playing pinball with me.

With a low count of seniors this year, my fellow junior class teammates and I have taken on the responsibility of setting respectable examples for the lower-classmen and making their soccer experience both fun and successful.

Looking forward to a fantastic season, I can't wait for the first home game. One, because there's no better feeling than your own turf under your cleats and two, because I can't wait to see the spark of that first game light up in the eyes of my newer teammates.

So, stock up on the Tide, Mom, and get out your old mud-scraping screwdriver, Dad. Proud smiles, high-fives, and "Go Streaks!" cheering can only mean one thing ... soccer season has begun!

Finals Bloom into Spring

MARCH 15

- -

WARNING: FINALS MAY CAUSE CRAMPING OF THE HANDS, SPLITTING headaches and uncontrollable yawning. If any student experiences these symptoms, have no fear; Spring Break is almost here!

Soon we will notice the birds chirping, flowers blooming, and me, well I'll be. . .sleeping, in only a matter of days. After finals week, the only things I feel like studying are the insides of my eyelids.

Although sleeping is a top priority on my spring "to-do" list, it isn't the only activity in which my classmates and I will happily participate.

Many of my friends and their families use Spring Break to catch up with each other on a relaxing vacation. My friend Ben is heading south to Branson, Missouri to spend some quality time hanging out with his family. Hot spots like Cancun and Florida are especially popular among my fellow breakers who like to skip spring altogether and belly flop right into summer. I'll be heading southwest, Phoenix to be exact.

Five fun-filled days cheering on my brother's college baseball team along with my parents is sure to be a blast. I know 45 - 50 innings of baseball on wooden bleachers eating dust may not sound ideal, but I know there will be a shopping trip in the cards if I keep a smile plastered to my face and a whine off my lips. I've also heard Arizona is the home of some sweet golf courses. However, I think the only club I'd need is my sand wedge.

Spring Break also is the perfect time of year to reunite with some recent GHS alumni. My teammates and I were excited when a few of our veterans came back to scrimmage with us at soccer practice this week. What an awesome gift it was to play with Kiara, Sade, Katie and Molly again, especially after they've gotten some college soccer experience under their cleats. I've also spotted some graduates talking to their former teachers in the hallways. My biology teacher, Mr. Allison, encourages his students to bring in colorful felt pennants representing the college they attend. . .I think he needs an NYU pennant to add to his collection around the room.

Our awesome Galesburg Marching Streaks are traveling to Disney World in Orlando, Florida to perform and enjoy the sights and sounds during a well-deserved vacation. Boy, I would love to be a fly on the wall in one of the charter buses around hour twenty-one. Go Band!

Most athletes look forward to Spring Break because it gives them a chance to totally focus on whatever the sport they are gearing up for. Balancing academics and athletics can be tough at times, so when there is a break in the studying action, I'm always relieved to play without worrying about taking a tricky trigonometry test the next day. If I'm lucky enough, I'll be able to comfortably balance my favorite sport, a family vacation, fun with friends, and sleeping late, all in one week.

Spring Break. Hitting the pillows instead of the books since the 1990s. Hey, Mother Nature, could you tone down on all that chirping and blooming for just one more week?

Praising Arizona

MARCH 22

- -

PLANES, SHUTTLE BUSES AND RENTAL CARS. LIKE RECENT MODES OF transportation, my daily routine this past week has been anything but "the usual." Sunday morning at about 8:30, I ditched my worn-out winter coat and clogs for shorts and green flip flops as I stepped onto the dry Arizona soil. The only things I knew about Arizona were Diamondbacks baseball and how close the nearest mall was to each ballpark in Phoenix.

Our first stop was the car rental center where we became the proud, temporary owners of a slick, 2008 P.T. Cruiser. I think my dad took the "Cruiser" part a little too literally, especially after whizzing by the first few Mustangs. I've never been so happy to see a parking lot!

As a golfer and soccer player, I felt out of my element in a place where grass was as scarce as a stain-free shirt on a 2-year- old. I beamed like the Arizona sun when I saw the par three golf course next door to our hotel. Of course, my "praise the grass dance" only lasted a few moments before it was back to the crazy Cruiser to scoot to my brother's baseball game. So, with turf-stained knees and oh-so stylish "plane hair," I stumbled back into the car with Daryl Waltrip behind the wheel.

Now, many of you know I am not the biggest baseball fan, but when I got out of the car and began to calculate the Jane-to- baseball player ratio, let me just say, from then on, I was always the first one to the car in the morning!

Seriously, I don't know if it was because I understood the game better or because I had gotten too much sun, but for the first time I was sincerely interested in watching the games. The most entertaining aspect of baseball I've grown to love is the hilarious dugout banter. Some of those ball players could give Jerry Seinfeld a run for his money. Nicknames like

"Truckosaurus," "Cupcake," "J.V. Gravy," and "Johnny Simp" provided some light-hearted laughs during many a rough and dusty game.

Eventually, we got to take a little break from baseball. So, my dad and brother went to a Cubs game while my mom and I did what we do best - hello, Scottsdale Fashion Square Mall! According to a couple of Phoenix natives, this particular mall was an ideal place for spotting celebrities. So, after four productive hours of shopping, my mom and I picked out the perfect place for celebrity sightings - the Starbucks next to the valet pickup. Although we saw more look-a-likes than real-life starlets, there were a couple of professional athletes, and one member of a band which will go unnamed until I can Google the lyrics he was proudly singing to the valet.

As my week of cacti, almost famous look-a-likes, and endless baseball came to a halt, I'll admit it was difficult to leave the sun. Saying so long to my brother (who had a bad case of Montezuma's Revenge while we were there) also made it tough to go. However, after a draggy double header in 85-degree weather, all I can say is, there's no place like home.

Breaking into Spring Despite the Weather

MARCH 29

- -

MY CALENDAR TELLS ME THAT SPRING HAS SPRUNG, BUT MOTHER Nature seems to think otherwise. I am still wearing traces of the Phoenix sun, but no one would notice because of the umpteen layers covering me up at our first soccer game.

Earmuffs, parkas, mittens and piles of "Under Armor" collecting on top of the radiator was a sight I wasn't expecting to see over vacation. Where has the sun been hiding lately? These past few weeks, my warm, old, brilliant pal has been lost behind a steady parade of rain, sleet and snow clouds, stacked up in our atmosphere like ants on a Jolly Rancher. When faced with such gloomy weather during what promised to be a time of fun and relaxation, I have two choices: let Old Man Winter get the best of me or create my own brand of Spring Break sunshine.

1. Laugh: There's nothing like telling a good joke to brighten up my day or put a chuckle on someone else. Smiles are contagious and serve as the perfect anecdote for the rainy weather blues. Whenever arctic temperatures keep me inside, it helps to pop in a favorite comedy or catch up on the "funnies" section of the newspaper ("For Better or Worse" is my personal favorite). If nothing else, there are always "Golden Girl" reruns!

2. Play: Experts say that exercise produces endorphins which can help improve a person's mood. Now, I'm not suggesting an indoor marathon, but why not make good use of that YMCA membership and challenge a friend to some "one-on-one" or a riveting match of racquetball? For those who are more into the individual fitness activities, here's a chance to bust out that summer suit and go for a brisk swim at the local municipal pool. Show off that Arizona tan before it fades into the oblivion of April. Yoga and Pilates also serve as a great way to stay active without having to hunt in the basement for those cross-country skis or bob and weave through an ice puddled jog.

3. Relax: Take a chill pill! Host a personal spa day by soaking neck-deep in a bubble bath, listening to soothing music or simply by kicking back into an afternoon cat nap. Everyone needs to let loose her inner couch potato now and then. Grab a handful of that Easter candy (even if someone else hunted for it) and become one with the TV Guide. For dinner, treat those taste buds to some serious comfort food such as chicken noodle soup, hot chocolate - the works.

Above all, I've learned that even though it may be called "Spring Break," that doesn't mean I can't pretend its still winter. Mother Nature sure seems to be doing just swell in that department!

Benefits of Giving Blood Outweigh the Turnoffs

APRIL 5

I DO NOT LIKE BLOOD. I NEVER ATE "COUNT CHOCULA" CEREAL, I refuse to even look at a bat cave, and I turn down every chance I get to wear fangs. That's right, no ketchup on my hot dog, either. Whether it's a paper cut or a measly scraped shin, I've never been a huge fan of the oozy red stuff, especially when it's exiting my own body. Obviously, it is a good idea I'm not in charge of the GHS Student Council blood drive this year! But, after learning more about the Red Cross and the benefits of giving blood to benefit someone in desperate need, I've become very supportive of the whole shebang.

Picking out my favorite animal sticker after getting shots at the pediatrician was fantastic back in the day. If it weren't for those fun "badges of honor," I'd never have made it to the front desk of the doctor's office. What's great about the blood drive is that donors can receive their own "badges of honor" without even stepping foot inside a pediatrician's office. Cool T-shirts are awarded to each person who gives his time and a pint of life-saving fluid to the nice nurses and other Red Cross folks.

Let's face it, people are attracted to food, especially growing teens like myself. Hang out a free food sign and get out of the way. Another awesome aspect of participating in the blood drive is that after their donation, volunteers get to munch on free juice and cookies. The last time I received treats after getting a shot, I was learning my ABC's and spelling words like "cat." Oh, the good old days!

What I find most exciting about donating blood is how one donation at GHS can save the life of someone on the other side of the country. Who knows? Perhaps that highly valued pint of GHS silver and gold will someday be typed and matched for a trendy high school student in California.

As far as the whole needle-phobia goes, according to my peers who are donating veterans, the whole process goes by in a snap, and the environment is anything but uncomfortable.

Unfortunately, I will not be able to participate at the GHS Blood Drive this year because of a soccer game. Shucks. But I do look forward to signing up to donate in the future. After all the positive feedback I've learned, maybe I should sign up to be on the blood drive committee, too! The annual blood drive will take place in the GHS learning center from 1:15-5:30 p.m. on Monday, April 7. Donator requirements can be found on any flyers around the school. I highly encourage all my fellow class-mates to make a real effort to sign up. Keep in mind, donating one hour of your time can ensure someone else's lifetime. Give it up!

It's a Digital World

APRIL 12

I'M NOTHING BUT A NUMBER.

It all started off last Friday when I received my first set of license plates. Cruising through the GHS parking lot, I have noticed a few clever plates. It's amazing what witty signatures my fellow classmates have cre-ated with just seven numbers and letters. Take for instance, my pal who came up with the car stamp CAMBOB1 or the GHS chemistry teacher displaying AG N AU for our beloved silver and gold. My brother, John, who trademarked his Monte Carlo with his baseball nickname and num-ber using SKINS10. Unfortunately, my dad decided not to spring for the vanity plates when it came to old Black Pearl, just a mish mash of letters and numbers that screams, "Ignore me!" Thus, my clever ideas of how to fit my name, favorite color, athletic numbers and birth date using seven characters remained just those, ideas.

The numerical pilgrimage did not stop there. This past Monday my teammates and I matched up against Washington on their home turf. With no wins yet recorded, we were hungry to stick the ball in the net. It wasn't until the 73rd minute of the game that we were able to score the only goal of the game. After a 1-0 finish, we were elated to have gotten the goose egg off the win column and grasp our first victory as a team. I suppose one isn't such a lonely number after all.

One and seven were my dynamic duo of digits for Tuesday due to the celebration of my 17th birthday. Considering my busy schedule and the misfortune of my day of days falling on a school night this year, I chose to celebrate with my three closest amigos: my mom, my dad and my dog. After gorging on a sweet slab of the Rib Shack's finest, it was time to bust out the cake. Despite the rainy weather, my family and I were able to keep the candles lit until I made my birthday wish. Two singers and one howler accompanied the 17 candles, 17 pieces of cake and 17 wonderful years of life.

And then there was the ACT. The ZAPS workshop replaced the normal schedule for many of my fellow juniors and me this past Wednesday. The objective was to learn how to "outsmart" the ACT by picking up a few helpful hints from the pros at ZAPS. Never in my life have I seen so many numbers, and I'm not just talking about the math section. Nearly every number in the 20s appeared in my score at the end of my sample tests (A perfect ACT score is 36 ... sigh). At the end of the day, I left the workshop with a new confidence about test-taking strategies to use on April 23 and 24 when all juniors will take the test at GHS.

Numbers, numbers everywhere. I've found them hidden in bumper tags, winning scores, birthdays, and especially standardized tests. As for a pearly plate idea, how does JNRZ 172 sound? Hey dad, who's your number one daughter?

Hair Today, Gone Tomorrow

APRIL 19

- -

IT WAS THE BEST OF HAIR DAYS, IT WAS THE WORST OF HAIR DAYS.

A morning of stressful tresses can influence my attitude toward the other 17 hours of the day. My most crucial question of style will always lead up to this, curly or straight? Or in Jane's world, would I rather resemble a poodle in a wind tunnel or walk around with fried, pancake-flat hair? I'll admit that I'm sometimes more concerned about what's on my head rather than what's in it. However, hair is a universal accessory that appears differently on each of its owners. Lately, I've recognized my fellow class-mates by how they individually manage their manes.

Hair is the one of the few features we can instantly transform. My teammates and I throw our intricate curls and signature school day styles into a messy bun or ponytail for the soccer field in a blink of an eye. Or perhaps, when the swimmers disguise their wacky, chlorine-damaged hair under a bald, black swim cap before a race and then ceremoniously have their long, starchy locks shaved off to prepare for post season competition.

Speaking of instantaneous transformation, how about that hair dye? After the now historically hysterical coloring incident of 2007, when I went from brassy orange to licorice black locks quicker than anyone can say "Halloween," I vowed to leave my hair color to the professionals. Let's just say, do-it-yourself-dye can turn into quite the "hairy" situation!

Then there are students who are known by their "signature cut." Dynamite Do's, such as the Afro, have been around for decades; yet, there are only a select few Streaks who choose to 'fro it up. The mullet is another famous style that can be worn well, or not so well, under certain circumstances - "business in the front, party in the back."

Today's popular haircuts for girls involve a slightly edgier version of the bob. The boys, on the other hand, tend to aim for what I'd call the "ski-jump," you know, the one with the little flip at the end. Some of the guys, it seems, are shooting for more Surf 'n Turf look of Joe Beach mixed with the all too familiar, ducktail. Bangs, an old fallback position, are another happening style for a lot of my friends, including myself.

Getting my hair all done up for a dance is often a nerve-wracking situation. Updos, downdos, half up half down dos. . .there's a never-end-ing list of dance do's, not to mention a few don'ts. It's difficult to choose which one goes best with the dress.

Hairstyles on the out include Stooges hair (the "Moe," "Larry," or "Curly"), crewcuts and Mohawks. Of course, there are the infamous bad hair days that include such unfortunate events as cowlicks, bed head, frizz, alarm clock-failed head, caphead and plain ole deflation.

For me, it's often a "tail" of two hair days. The morning's typical layered shag or the Jane, you are going to be late for school curls, curls, curls. Oh no, is it raining? Where's my scrunchie?

Test Tests More than Smarts

APRIL 26

- -

ACT TESTING BEGAN PRECISELY AT 7:45 A.M. ON WEDNESDAY MORN-ing. At approximately 7:44 a.m., I sprinted down the English hallway, hooked a right at the foreign language wing, just barely making it in time to take my seat. There's nothing like a good run before a mind jog!

After I caught my breath, I reached for my testing gear: a couple of number two pencils, TI-34 calculator and a brightly colored safety pin wrist-watch (fashion helps me focus). I glanced around at my test mates, some obviously shaking in their flip-flops. A few chewed on their Papermates while others tapped them repetitively on their desktops. Of course, there were those cool as a cucumber students with their feet up underneath the desk in front of them like they were watching the Cubs game at home. Although nervous, most of my fellow classmates looked well rested. There was no bed head or raccoon eyes to be found that morning.

As far as the exam itself, it looked just like all my other tests. My timed writing essay looked like Egyptian hieroglyphics. I mistyped on my calculator so frequently, the "undo" button will be forever embedded into the keypad like the impression of a fossilized T-Rex. During the sci-ence portion, I'm surprised I didn't start my own experiment on the flam-mability caused by the continual friction of my eraser on the paper.

There was also a noticeable amount of sounds I picked up on Wednesday morning. For instance, everyone in my testing room was given a piece of candy to consume during the exam; however, it became slightly more of a distraction than a focus aid. Have you ever been in a movie theater when the person behind you proceeded to chomp obnoxiously loud on his popcorn? Well, that's the same annoying feeling I harbored during the first five minutes of Wednesday's test. But, beyond the momentary car alarm and gum smacking, GHS was the quietest it's ever been. As a matter of fact, it was apparent by the occasional growling sound in front of me that somebody had missed breakfast.

At the end of the day, the ACT ended up quizzing more than my smarts. It also tested my patience. Depending on how my scores turn out, maybe next time I'll pack ear plugs and a visor as my own personal focus aids! It probably wouldn't hurt to be early next time either.

ACT Question 35: If Jane sprints down the 200-foot English hallway at 45 mph and has 10 seconds to make it to class, will she be late?

A. Depends on the shoes. She slides in safely in Nikes but doesn't make it to first in flip-flops.

B. Its impossible, Jane's top speed is 10 mph with a 5-mph tailwind.

C. Yes, unless that new guy in school is at his locker.

D. Forget it, at 45 mph she'll miss the turn at the foreign language wing and end up like yesterday's homework assignment - smeared on the French room blackboard!

Active Learning is Fashionable

MAY 3

LEARNING IS LIKE FASHION. THERE IS A VAST VARIETY OF STYLES, AND people discover through trial and error what works best for them.

I am an active learner. There is only so much sitting and listening I can take until the classroom morphs into "Planet Jane" and I completely space out. However, if my teacher throws in a little class activity, I'll be as alert as a mom hunting in the newspaper for buy-one, get-one-free coupons.

Take, for instance, my freshman year Honors English class. We could've been reading about dry wall and I guarantee Ms. Sheryl Hinman would have made it the "talk of the teens." Thanks to her inventive ideas and fun projects, participating in English class became the highlight of my day.

I can remember being introduced to Greek mythology during freshman year. I never put the "fan" in fantasy, nor did I have an apt appreciation for science-fiction in general. The only knowledge I had of Hercules resulted from repeatedly watching an animated Disney movie. It wasn't until I enrolled in Ms. Hinman's English class that I realized the fascination of Greek mythology. While studying the Greek gods, my fellow classmates and I were assigned a project where we would break into groups and develop our own cultures. Culture presentations would involve everything from laws to religions created from our own ideas. I couldn't recall the last time I had embraced any sort of science-fiction related material with such an open mind.

Ms. Hinman will retire at the end of this year. Thanks, Mrs. H, for dusting off our imaginations and goofiness that so many of us kept in hiding during our "Did he just look at me?" junior high years.

Another class that keeps me in action mode is American Studies. I should start wearing a pedometer considering I probably get my 10,000 steps a day after first period. Although, if not for the upbeat atmosphere and fun in-class assignments, I'm sure I'd have a lot more Q's than A's. My favorite task is designing picket signs for different strikes and protests that occurred throughout the decades. I love coming up with catchy, often humorous phrases, while admiring the creativity of my fellow history buffs. For example, when a couple of my classmates gave a project on Apollo 13, we were asked to create picket signs supporting additional funding for the space program, as though we were living in the year 1968. "Skip the stars, reach for the moon," was just one of many ingenious slogans created by my peers.

Active learning is like riding a bike. You've got to pedal fast to get going, but the more you move, the stronger the breeze becomes … .and I don't mean between your ears.

Summer No Longer Time for Slacking

MAY 10

- -

IN MY FORMER, CAREFREE YEARS OF ADOLESCENCE, THOUGHTS OF summer vacation revolved around the three S's: swimming, sunbathing and sleeping-in. That was back in my innocent years before I was told about the fourth S, the guy that keeps coming up in conversation at the Simkins dinner table since the Black Pearl arrived and before senior year, Mr. Sweat.

I can remember my first summer job. I didn't need an application or a driver's license. As a matter of fact, I got paid over the minimum wage of any 8-year-old I knew. Unfortunately, when applying for a job that requires skills beyond manipulating a garden hose in proper fashion, watering my dad's flowers doesn't count as prior work experience.

Yes, my dreams of a responsibility-free vacation were erased from my imagination when my parents dropped the J-O-Bomb on me a couple of months ago. After a couple of applications here and there, I was still floating in the same income boat when I got the "gas money = Jane's piggy bank" speech, lost and jobless. Eventually, I began thinking about where my friends were working and asked them for some experienced employment advice.

Friend Maria is currently holding two positions, one at the Galesburg Recreation Center and another at O.N. Custer baseball park as a concessions manager. Upon hearing her already scheduled-out summer, I inquired as to how she went about finding these great opportunities. Basically, she advised me to take a trip to the unemployment office, fill out some forms, and simply start applying myself. According to my procrastination clock, I'll be sure to begin sending out my apps within a few days. Before I apply, I'll need to figure out what jobs would put my best skills to use.

Many of my fellow classmates are spending their summers under the sun at the local swimming holes, saving lives and preventing horseplay around the perimeters of the pools. Lifeguarding is a summer job staple. Then there are those who will be serving in the fast food industry, encouraging others to "eat fresh" or to keep on "lovin' it." There are also a fortunate few who will enjoy restocking shelves and providing a "helpful smile in every aisle" while toiling at one of our local groceries. Of course, who can forget the good ol' baby-sitting days? Playing dolls or racing mini-monster trucks with youngsters is always a fun throwback, but I'm not sure I could handle three straight months of it.

So, whether I'm serving up your steak, bagging your bananas, or pulling you out of the deep end, I just hope to discover a way to pay for those summer expenditures, also known as fuel. The next time you see me, I might be the one in the window asking, "Would you like fries with that?" If not, maybe that birthday money can at least buy me a new pair of walking shoes.

Sports Banquet 'Golden' Moment
MAY 17

"THANK YOU FOR BEING A FRIEND, TRAVEL DOWN THE ROAD AND back again. ..." Whenever I hear those familiar lyrics calling to me from the television, I'm tuned in for the next 30 minutes to four elderly women making witty wisecracks about life and just being old. I'm still in my teens, but my favorite way to spend a half hour is watching Lifetime reruns of the "Golden Girls."

One funny characteristic I've picked up from the series is how food becomes more of a focal point in life as we get older. Whether it's Rose, Blanche, Dorothy, or even Sophia having a minor hair, money, medical, or man crisis, she's off to her battle station, in other words ... the fridge. Whether it's cake, ice cream, or both, the girls always solve their problems over a plate of food. As a matter of fact, nearly half of the "Golden Girls" scenes are set in the kitchen.

Speaking of eating with a bunch of friends, this Sunday will be our annual girl's soccer banquet at Soangetaha Country Club. Banquets are always a spectacular way to end the season on a good note. Coaches provide speeches of a job well done and present players with MVP awards, record-holding medals, conference awards, and the precious, most improved player distinction. There's no doubt the captains love individually handing out "gag gifts" to each of their teammates, each recognizing a hilarious memory or quirky personality trait. I remember receiving a pair of vampire teeth in honor of my infamous pair of pop-outable canines at one of our past golf banquets.

Before the speeches and gift-giving, there's the one question that's always in the back of everyone's mind, what's for dinner?

With three years of banquets under, and perhaps over, my belt, I believe I've got the whole dining system under wraps. Seniority rules. The older athletes usually attack the salad bar before the lowerclassmen can get a plate in edgewise. Then follows the families and coaches, who somehow always end up with the guys in the front of the line while the girls patiently wait their turn. Then there's the whole "to go for round two, or to not go for round two," question that many banquet attendees experience. How to take advantage of high-quality leftovers without appearing piggish - that's a pickle, no pun intended.

Oftentimes, there will be dessert to follow the main course, usually consisting of sugar cookies in the shape of soccer balls or baseballs, whichever sport applies. This is often a reassurance to the person asking himself or herself the "round two" question. This way, if they're still hungry but fear others will find them selfish or greedy, they know there are cookies in the corner waiting to temporarily inflate the waistline like bike tires.

Of course, for some it's all about appearance. These paranoid few pass through round one of the salad bar, limiting their portions to sizes even mice would find skimpy, then reluctantly nibble at their cookie while slyly shoveling table mints and bits of confetti into their purses. These, my friends are the group of people I like to call the "Golden Girls," because you know that come midnight, they'll be kicking themselves for holding back at dinner and head directly for their battle stations.

Life Lessons to Take You Over the Next Hill

MAY 24

- -

I AM SITTING OUTSIDE OF HEGG AUDITORIUM THURSDAY AFTER school sorting Project Graduation T-shirts according to size. In the meantime, members of the GHS class of 2008 are on the other side of the wall, rehearsing for graduation which will be held this Sunday afternoon. Hmmm…I wonder if this would be a good time to share some words of wisdom I've stumbled across this past week?

Last Saturday, I attended my brother's graduation from Macalester College in St. Paul. The commencement speaker was Macalester grad Peter Berg, producer of Friday Night Lights and the new Will Smith movie, Hancock. There were no clichéd comparisons of "opening another chapter in the book of life," or quoting of Webster's dictionary. Instead, Mr. Berg spoke to the graduates as if he was chatting it up at a barbeque with a root beer and a baseball game playing in the background. In his casual fashion, he kept repeating the same words of advice to make sure every graduate would remember, "Never let anyone push you around" and every once in a while, "Lay down, close your eyes, and breathe." Somewhere between the "Congrats Grad" cake, dressing up Grandma Shirley in John's cap and gown, and blinding camera flashes, it hit me. In just one year, this would be me, tossing my cap in the air amidst my classmates and, soon after beginning my slow and steady climb from the bottom of the academic totem pole once again. Was I going to let the "big dogs" push me around? Would I raise my hand in a class of names and faces I didn't recognize? I'll get back to you, I think I need to lie down.

After retreating from the Twin Cities, the inspirational messages continued at our Student Council banquet (yes, another banquet). After the meal, we celebrated the awesome seniors, reflected on our achievements over the past year, and handed out nifty awards like the "Great Inventor" certificate. Our new student council advisor, Mr. Schaafsma, challenged us to "observe the culture of our school." We also had the chance to chat with fellow Stu Co members and their families while snacking on

Student Council cake (Golden Girls flashback). After sharing the story of my brother's scary encounter with a deer on the interstate on his drive home Monday night, I was given a life-saving piece of advice by Jenelle's dad. "Jane, if a deer runs in front of you while driving, do not swerve."

Immediately following the banquet, we gathered at our home with family and my parents' friends, to celebrate my dad turning 50 years old. Perhaps the best gifts, besides great company, were the inspirational, yet witty birthday cards. One of my favorites read, "It's your 50th birthday? Well, don't just stand there…At least, not without some assistance!" Of course, my dad enjoyed the line, "You're not getting older, you're getting cooler!" Then there was my card, "Happy Over the Hill Day Dad!" Hey, we can't all be Shakespeares.

Well, as it turned out, the seniors took longer to practice than I expected, so I was unable to stay and share my offerings of life lessons. So, if there are any seniors out there reading this, I say to you, "Stay on the road, don't let anyone misdirect you, and look forward to what is waiting for you over the hill. Congratulations!

Juniors in the Driver's Seat

MAY 31

IT'S 10:30 P.M. THURSDAY AND I AM COMPOSING MY FINAL COLUMN of the school year. Gee, one would think a senior in high school would learn not to wait until the last. . .hold the phone, did I just refer to myself as a senior? I think someone just mailed me a reality check.

The day has finally come. The day that you wake up and find yourself counting down your remaining high school time in days rather than years. The day that the weird-looking '09 on your letter jacket suddenly becomes all too real. The day when all those upperclassmen have fled the scene and left you in the driver's seat on an open road.

Thank goodness for summer break to get used to the steering and brakes on this odd vehicle called senior year. Come September, senior reality will begin to sink in fast as heavy traffic appears on the horizon;

better grab the wheel tightly to stay out of the ditch and headed in the right direction. Just one year in the distance there'll be no backseat drivers waking you with motivational morning anthems like "get up, or you'll be late for school."

Perhaps, I'll title the post high-school years in my life something more scholarly and sophisticated than "Jane's Journal," maybe something along the lines of "The Chronicles of Jane." Yes, I suppose "chronicles" sounds slightly more mature. Yikes! Listen to me already using extensively, over-the-top terminology. Yeesh, I sound like I skipped senior year, and went straight through my first term of college English. Let's slam it into "park" a second and take a gander out the back window to a great junior year.

Though it was my third year at GHS, this older dog still learned some new tricks. With the help of classes like American Studies, I discovered GHS has some very creative teachers. By trying out for cheerleading, I taught myself to continue taking chances, even if I can't do a back flip. I also found out how hard I'll have to work just to get B's in some classes. Thanks to classes like trigonometry and French 3, I've been instructed to study every night, and not just the day before a test. For now, I'll have to put my dreams of Ivy Leagues on hold. However, I'm sure an introductory trip to New York City would ease my desire of attending an east coast college...for now.

Besides exploring foreign campuses, senior year brings with it the "R-word." Responsibility. Now I'm not talking about the kind of responsibility my parents use when I forget to water the plants. This responsibility is all about taking ownership of leadership qualities. For instance, as a senior, the whole "class-clown" act has reached its closing curtain. Take a bow back of the classroom, chuckling chums, exit stage left, and leave the lame bathroom jokes to the underclassmen. Of course, keep the humor alive, just not to that breaking point where it crosses the line from an occasional witty remark to, "See me after class." Be proud to be a Silver Streak. Take honor in our school and enjoy our last year in it. Never went out for the team and regret it? Do it. It's never too late to get involved in a squad, club, or any school activity for that matter.

What it comes down to, my fellow class of 2009, is this. Let's hold our heads up high and make our last year at GHS supercalifragilisticexpialidocious!

SENIOR YEAR

Summer Soundtrack a Different Beat

AUGUST 30

- -

I burned a new CD yesterday. Unfortunately, I won't be able to sing along in the Black Pearl or download it onto my MP3 player. As a matter of fact, it's not even on a disc. No worries though, I can listen to it whenever and wherever I feel the urge to jam.

Oh, the soundtrack of my summer. Topping my play list is a tune written by two close pals, Sean and Shelby, not to be mistaken with Sonny and Cher. About three days a week, I had the privilege (according to them) to "big-kid-sit" through the morning and early afternoon. Opening my eyes and oftentimes ears to a new sound each day, I had a blast marching to the beat of a drummer other than myself. Their songs are quite popular, maybe you've heard of them?

"Are we there yet?"… "5 more minutes!"… and my favorite, "Oops, I did it again." Though I'm glad to be heading off to college next summer, I will miss making music with my two mini-maestros.

Up next on the playlist, I bring you a song with a slightly more intense beat than the first. When not playing Hide and Go Seek or doctoring up a bowl of Colossal Crunch Berries, I was busy constructing a make-shift gym in the garage. AC/DC has nothing on my "heavy metal." After hauling in one yoga ball, two free weights, a plastic jump rope, a chalk-drawn calisthenics ladder, and a Pilates mat that doubled as an oil spill cover up, I no longer needed a membership at the local gym.

Track 3 has more of an opera feel. Opera in the sense that while driving through Chicago traffic in a vain attempt to make a 9 a.m. Lake Forest College visit, my dad bellowed like Pavaroti when we met the 30-car traffic jam. And, like listening to an Italian opera, my parents and I were completely oblivious as to what language the professor was speaking while visiting an Elizabethan art class that same day.

The final tune is a familiar, yet unexpected one, with a theme that's in a category all its own. Instrumentals include lots of bells, a marching band in the background, and the sound of chalk scaling a chalkboard. The lyrics are unique, yet recognizable. "What lunch do you have?" "Test tomorrow over Chapter 1 ..." "Quit sticking your gum under my desk!" "My dog ate it ..." Ah yes, I remember what this class of music is called - the good ol' Schoolhouse Rock!

Electing to Tap the 'Inner Self'

SEPTEMBER 6

- -

FLIPPING THROUGH THE COURSE CATALOG AT THE END OF JUNIOR year, I felt a freedom to customize my senior year with a course or two that provoke personal interest. Will Horse Management spin my spurs? Do I want to hook, line and sink 'em in Outdoor Living? Or perhaps, Auto Mechanics will spark my engine? Don't get me wrong, requirements for college remain high on my list, yet I also feel "required" to tap into my inner Jane as well.

One week into Drawing One, I feel like a fly at a pie convention, constantly in awe of my surroundings, a bit messy, enjoying every last morsel. Our first assignment was to test our shading techniques by replicating still-life geometric shapes and the shadows they created. Although my precisely angled cube resembled more of a beaten-up Fed-Ex package, I was reassured by my fellow starving artists that my spheres put their cones to shame.

After washing off the ebony smudges from my hands, I got my fingers and mind better acquainted with the P.C. in Computer Concepts. Looking towards a career in media communications, I was excited to be able to scrunch a technology course into my schedule. Much to my satisfaction, I've already been able to design a few event flyers allowing me to use my creativity and discover techniques that have enhanced my savvy with the computer a macro-load. That's techie lingo for a bunch.

Across the hall, I enter a world that combines creative thinking with rules and structure. The grueling, yet invaluable class that is College Writing. Despite having learned of a deadly thesis paper headed my way, I was keen about expanding my extensive vocabulary incalculably and enhancing my writing skills, no matter the price. Besides, there's nothing I love more than waking up to the superior challenge of a thesis paper that sounds like it could make the Oxford English Dictionary look like a Post-It Note.

Stopping to catch my breath after College Writing, I took a seat next to my pal Olivia for the fascinating universe of theories and experimentation that awaited us in Physics I. Calculus may have taken a backseat on my schedule this year, but I wasn't about to let all sense of mathematics slip away. On the first day, without hesitation, Mr. Baxter got us off our seats and into a scientific project before you could say, "beakers and goggles." Much to my surprise, there were no test tubes or glass bottles of any kind within sight. Instead, a computer and a classic battery powered car stood in front of us. The strategy was to measure out various distances of travel using a meter stick to record how long it took the buggy to travel from point A to point B. Who knew graphing could be so fun!

Senior year has kicked off with a few minor glitches. My locker was stuck on more than one occasion (thank you Mr. Hoosen), my lunch has changed from C, to A, to D (there is a D lunch?), and I hit the wrong golf ball at our first home meet. But the fact that I can drift into an art class first thing in the morning and draw my troubles away, makes this senior happy as a gaptoothed girl walking home from school with her buckeye-chucking brother.

Jane is Not Dumb ... or Shy

SEPTEMBER 13

THE IRONY OF IT ALL . . .

I began taking piano lessons at the ripe old age of 6 and continued tickling the ivories until I was about 10. Whether I was playing Beethoven's

"9th Symphony" for 50 people in a church, or "Chopsticks" via request from aunts and uncles, I always experienced a bad case of the nerves. As a matter of fact, it was common to "See Jane Run" after playing my musical selection at required recitals like Jackie Joyner Kersie in the 100-meter dash. I slammed my songbook shut as if I was hiding it from the CIA, then immediately ran off the stage with my eyes glued to the floor.

Seven years and a long talk with dad about stage etiquette later, the only thing I run away from now is high fives after PE class. And who would have guessed that I would hold the office of Corresponding Secretary for student council? Not only must I give weekly student council updates on the radio, but I also serve as student representative at monthly school board meetings.

Other than shyness, GHS has helped me clear the one academic hurdle that's always been a stretch for me - math. Mathematics brought back the memory of reading "Jane is dumb" etched on a chalkboard in second grade by some of my smarter classmates after I failed to solve a subtraction problem.

Ten years, two math tutors and a long talk with mom about boys later, I'm the first to volunteer my friend Olivia and myself when Mr. Baxter summons someone to the front blackboard to solve equations from our physics homework. Needless to say, no one has written, "Jane is dumb" on any chalkboards since. In fact, in my third-grade circle, I am known as the "Master of Multiplication."

This week, I added another life learning lesson from high school. I was able to share this achievement with my good friend, Maria, as we got the nerve to ask a couple of boys if they would "possibly consider" the idea of going with us to Homecoming. One "maybe" and "already taken" later, we recovered from the awkwardness and remain relentlessly optimistic in our search. Freshman year, if you would have told me I would not text, Facebook, or phone, but walk straight up to a boy and, face to face, ask him to a dance, I would have bolted away with my eyes glued to the linoleum in the school hallway.

Alas, GHS has taught me more than how to tiptoe in after the late bell and un-jam a stubborn locker. I've come a long way baby!

Post from Jane's Facebook page at age 27 (reflecting on the previous Journal entry)

17 years ago, I shrunk into my 2nd grade wooden desk, embarrassed and fuming as one of my classmates scribbled "Jane is dumb" on the chalkboard. The secret was out. I was bad at math. Thankfully, I have two stellar parents and a wicked smart brother who arranged tutoring sessions and stayed up into the wee hours of the night, helping me with Algebra 1A, 1B, trig, and geometry all the way through high school. Fast forward 17 years and I'm acing my graduate level stats class. It hasn't been easy, but by utilizing online educational resources like Khan Academy, I've been able to learn at my own pace. This morning, I received this photo from my parents who went to an open house at my old school. My super rad mother went into my old 2nd grade classroom and wrote "Jane is Smart" on the blackboard. So, to all you dumbies out there, this one's for you.

High School Survival Depends on Etiquette

SEPTEMBER 20

- -

ETIQUETTE, SHMETIQUETTE? I DON'T THINK SO!

Along with arriving to school on time and doing homework every night, student etiquette at GHS is vital for survival. Let me begin by laying out the rules of the road.

When walking down the hallways, one must stick to the right side at all times. If this rule alone is not obeyed, major complications are sure to follow. It is also important that one pays attention to the daily speed limits. Monday and Tuesday, corridor cruising speeds average roughly eleven classrooms per minute. However, as the week drags into and over "hump day," the limit tends to drop to about seven floor tiles per hour. As far as Friday goes, it's every man for himself! Warning, if one comes across a traffic jam or collision, please help the victims of the accident pick up their books, papers and selves.

Every coed loves lunch, but sometimes those late morning hunger pangs can spark a major L.R.C, Lunch Room Controversy. First rule, one must never, ever cut in front of another luncher. Even if one's best friend supposedly saved him a spot in line, he will have to patiently wait for his chicken nuggets like everyone else. When it comes to seating arrangements, tables will usually fit eight to nine people per side, comfortably. Double-digit elbowroom leads to double-trouble. Most importantly, however, is the golden rule of lunching. Never leave a man behind. One is not to sit alone, unless he or she so desires or has just come from an over-competitive pickleball game in gym. Additionally, loner lunchers shall always be invited to the nearest group to chow down.

Up next, we're taking it to the streets. In order for one to become a responsible and respected parker in the GHS lots, it is necessary that said person respects all other mobiles, bikes included. If one is not confident they can fit, quit. Never underestimate the limited space created by vans and pick up trucks. The light poles keep near-sighted extracurriculars from hitting other nighttime objects, like the Black Pearl, so refrain from treating them as parking blocks during the day. Also, those numbered spaces aren't there for decoration, just keep away. Ignorance of this etiquette is no excuse, resulting in towing, fines, and one very unhappy gym teacher!

What's that sound I hear? It's the Fashion Police, and they're on the prowl. The three fashion laws in the GHS Code of Conduct sound like a game of "Bop It": belt it, button it, or zip it. As far as girls' apparel goes, keep the straps about an inch or so thick and leave the "spaghetti" to Chef Boyardee. All I have to say to the boys is, keep the Levis level.

Although these guidelines can seem overwhelming, life in the halls of GHS will proceed smoothly by simply keeping this etiquette motto in mind: "Right, invite, light, and not too tight!"

Of Courses and Courses

SEPTEMBER 27

AS A PROUD MEMBER OF THE GALESBURG GIRLS' GOLF TEAM THE past four years, I am finally beginning to realize how much this sport means to me. From the talented and hilariously fun teammates to the all-too-familiar "keep your chin up" after another less-than-successful round, it's been both a blast and a real character-builder. But recently, I have also noticed how golf has introduced nifty ways to transfer my skills from the greens into the grade books.

Before approaching any shot, I have been instructed by Coach Gottenborg to line up my club with the pin. Although this method doesn't always keep me out of the sand traps, it never seems to penalize me in drawing class. Whether I'm painting an ocean landscape or sketching my favorite Disney character, golf has kept me staying inside the lines. In contrast, art classes have provided me with some creative tools to spiff up my golf game. Never again will I mistake another player's ball for my own, especially with red hearts and squiggles Sharpied onto all my Titleist No. 2s.

Plugging away in Computer Concepts, I am constantly reminded of the importance in improving the mental aspect of my golf game. I'm not sure that it's the monotonous green floor tiles or the sound of acorns catapulting from the trees outside that challenge my focus in class. With each misplaced stroke of the keyboard, the resulting misspelled word reminds me of nearly knocking out the parents who were tucked behind a tree during last week's match. If only I could take advantage of the "undo" button on the links.

Golf is a universal language. In fact, it is so ubiquitous I often use the words I hear (and repeat) on the course to expand my College Writing vocabulary. Except, of course, the ones I have learned while golfing with my dad. One term, in particular, has become such a staple of my golfing vocabulary that it has begun to carry over into my writing. "Fore!" on the fairways now shows up as foreboding, forlorn, foraging and everything but forgotten in my writing; the list of possibilities goes on forever. Even President Lincoln, obviously a golfing hack who knew how to deliver a good "fore" when the situation called for it, made clever use of the term by putting it ahead of his "score" in the infamous Gettysburg Address.

Playing at Lick Creek in Pekin on Thursday, I had the opportunity to put my physics formulas to work as well. As I came across the long par 5 known as the "Beast," I geared up with my troops, velocity and time. All it took was a little calculating and before I knew it, I had tamed the Beast with the army of acceleration.

As the year closes in on Western Big Six competition Monday, followed by regionals and, for some of my teammates, sectionals and beyond, I look forward to finding ways to enjoy the interrelationships of my game on the golf course with my courses at school. By keeping my chin up, using a little fore!sight, and occasionally staying clear of the rough (compliments of the undo button), life ahead promises to be nothing but fairways and greens.

Nothing Like Homecoming to Boost Energy

OCTOBER 4

- -

START YOUR DAY THE SILVER STREAK WAY WITH A CUP OF GHS Homecoming Hurrah! A combination of the best music, football, dancing and decorations, Homecoming Hurrah will give you that extra boost as summer fades into fall of your senior year.

If I concocted my own custom mix of Homecoming Hurrah, I would intersperse my most cherished memories from this week, beginning with my fellow Streaks golfers and me surprising everyone but us by coming home from a long Quincy trip with the hardware of a Western Big Six Tournament Championship. Another trophy worthy effort began last week with the ever amusing and fun activity of building the class float. There's nothing quite like stuffing thousands of tissue papers into the holes on a chicken-wired hayrack, all in the effort of creating a mobile masterpiece.

During the past couple of weeks, several of my fellow seniors and I spent our evenings at Emily's grandparents' farm engineering what is sure to "inch" it's way to a perfect 10 past the judging table. The only difficult aspect of float building has been keeping our idea a secret from under-cover, underclassmen spies. Hopefully, no imposters were able to "worm" their way into our low-profile construction site. However, it shouldn't be too difficult to identify the fingerprints in paint left behind.

Next up, I think I'll toss in some turf. It's hard to beat those Friday night lights, particularly on a "Neon Night." Speaking of hard to beat, I can't wait to cheer on our GHS football Streaks as they "devour the Devils" from Quincy. Adding on the layers while the wind whips at my face and the Streaks run that pigskin into the end zone is a feeling like no other. Outstanding halftime performances by our recently crowned grand champion marching band and always groovin' Gadets are sure to give my Homecoming Hurrah an extra "kick."

Somewhere between the pomping and the cheering, I'll have to refuel. I know just the place. It's the back of a truck, but not just any truck, the G-club, Pre-Game Tailgate Party truck! After all the "elbow, elbow, wrist, wrist" at the parade, there are sure to be some hungry athletes. In order to feed such a crowd, G-Club is grilling out for the annual tailgating party, providing free, pre-game grub for all varsity athletes. With all these competitors hanging around the Weber grill, I can only hope that Tailgate doesn't end in a hamburger-eating contest.

But of course, no cup of Homecoming Hurrah would be complete without a dash of dance. In a recent update, the inter-rotational date group has nearly tripled in size since I last wrote. Fluorescent decorations consisting of student council's spatter paintwork, shown off by the brilliance of black lights surrounding the dance floor, will truly turn John Thiel Gymnasium into a "Neon Night."

By Sunday morning, I'm sure I will wake up with tissue paper in my hair, spray paint on my hands, and a glow stick around my neck. However, with a quick sip of my Homecoming Hurrah, I'll be ready to take on the rest of my senior year ... even with a char-broiled, all beef patty cheese-burgered to my face.

College Selection No Easy Undertaking

OCTOBER 11

ACADEMIC YEAR: SENIOR. SECONDARY SCHOOL: GALESBURG HIGH School. Looking for: A private college with a media communications major, a Johnny Depp-good-looking baseball team, and preferably non-stinky dorm rooms. Is that so much to ask? "College hunting requires more than picture browsing through a brochure, Jane," my mom notifies me.

With the fabulous four-day weekend ahead, my parents and I decided to fly north to Naperville, IL Friday for round two of the college search. After visiting Lake Forest College earlier this summer, I feel prepared for whatever curveballs North Central College throws my way. With my dreams of an East Coast college in mind, Dad reminds me that these two schools fit nicely into his shortsighted description of "out east."

Visiting a school is like searching for your first home. The tour guide is the "Real 'em in" realtor, I'm the oblivious buyer, while Mom and Dad play the role of the fidgety financial advisors. However, there is quite a bit more to consider when the future of my education is on the line.

Much like a real-estate open house, the introduction at most college visits includes a short and sweet summary of the institute and what types of students best fit their school's personality. This is also the moment that sets the tone for the rest of the day's activities. But no matter how tasty the cafeteria food checks out, if a communications major is about as common as a panda bear roaming Lincoln Park, I may have to get lunch to go.

During the guided campus tours, I feel like the potential buyer again, walking through the house for the first time checking every room with a critical eye. Of course, I have yet to find any college campus unattractive, especially in the fall when the pathways on the "Quad" are lined with the amazing shades of autumn leaves. Campus tours are for more than just letting out the occasional "ooh" and "aah" at 19th century buildings. The guides usually use this time to fill in prospective students on campus activities, clubs, athletics, and the everyday life of a resident at their school while also avoiding parking blocks as they walk backwards on the paths.

The same way a realtor leaves the potential buyers with informational papers at the end of the tour, college visits never leave their potential students empty handed. I could have built a giant sequoia in my backyard with the stack of studying abroad literature, application tips, and an Ultimate Frisbee team sign- up sheet that somehow buried itself amongst the pile.

Last, but not least, as I have been reminded more than once by the financial advisors, is the price tag. Beyond the well-manicured lawns, ivy-covered walls, fabulous café, and guys with looks from the Depp-end of the gene pool, looms perhaps the biggest hurdle to putting the "Sold" sign in the school yard. There is an endless list of potential grants, scholarships, work study, and other tuition incentives that the Financial Aid Office ensures will follow you home in the mail in the days and weeks following the college visit. The trick is to put me in the college penthouse while keeping the folks out of the poorhouse. What's that, Dad? What do you mean, "my" loan?

Where have You Been?

OCTOBER 18

I'M ONE OF THOSE PEOPLE THAT WILL BE LATE TO MY OWN FUNERAL. No matter how early I wake up, something always manages to keep me sprinting to class like a mad woman. A last-minute wardrobe change has been my most recent delay dilemma as fall insists on layering my fashion. After almost an entire term of rushing into first block Drawing class within seconds of tardiness, I'm sure my classmates have begun a contest to see what day the tardy bell will finally beat me. Whether it's a Student Council meeting, homework assignment, or even a library book, I am always overdue.

Of course, I am not proud of my many belated arrivals. I would certainly rather symbolize the early bird than the running late loon. Nevertheless, there is one lesson I have learned from my hurry scurry ways; it is an art form all its own.

Art in the sense that there is a certain level of talent and creativity that one must acquire if arriving late is in the cards. Of course, this research has been acquired through extensive observations of my classmates, not myself (self-protection from parental interrogation later). For instance, the first question everyone asks when someone shows up after the bell is, "Where have you been?" This is the golden inquiry, but the answer is vital for survival. Especially if you are addressing the entire Law in America class.

After the big question is served, the key is to stay calm. Remain in a relaxed stance and refrain from any sort of twitching or loss of eye contact. Pupils darting around the room are a dead giveaway. Even more crucial to the unveiling of the excuse is the delivery. Hesitation is a sure-fire way to sure get fired.

At a loss for words? In case the real reason you were tardy has hitched a ride to Texas and flown south for the winter, just say the magic word, train. About 95 percent of the time, this excuse will pass with flying colors, given the many railroad crossings that intersect our Purington Pavers. However, there are some land mines to look out for when tiptoeing your way to freedom using the magic word. Be sure that there are in fact train tracks between your initial base and arrival area. If this problem occurs, both you and your geographic-wise teacher may realize you've reached your final destination.

If all else fails, speak the truth. Taking the path of integrity may result in a pink slip dropped into your honesty box, but at least it will exempt you from question number two. "The Amtrak stops at the mall?"

Power Rangers Didn't Require Mom

OCTOBER 25

- -

IT WAS 2ND GRADE, THE DAY OF THE HALLOWEEN PARADE AT SILAS Willard Elementary. From the cute little pug-nosed pig to the Flamenco-dancer to the hardly scary ghost, my mom had always insisted on constructing my annual, homemade costumes with whatever odds and ends were found lying around the house. To even glance at a manufactured "Scream" mask off the rack at Target would have been a sin at our house. So, it was no shock that in my third year of school that mom decided to put those Martha Stewart magazines to good use. Now, I'm not sure if it was my fault for insisting to be a cat or Mom's for being overly confident in her sewing skills, but whatever the reason, I was in for a major wardrobe malfunction.

It was a particularly hot day to be marching around the building, especially for a black cat. Mom was unable to make it to the parade, so Grandma Shirley stepped in to help me prepare my outfit. I hadn't noticed it before the parade began, but my home-sewn skirt was intent on slipping south for the fall. With one hand grasping my skirt for dear life, the other was busy inside its mitten removing the fuzzy fur that had founds its way to my mouth. By the turn of the second corner at Fremont and Seminary, I was ready to just let it go and hope that everyone would assume my tights were part of the costume. Luckily, I made it through every hallway, down every sidewalk and into my seat without becoming a hairless feline.

However, the best was still yet to come. After about thirty rounds of Heads Up Seven Up, I had unfortunately regained the confidence to walk without holding my skirt for dear life. Just as I headed for the cookie table, I suddenly felt a slight breeze behind me. But it was not until the roar of laughter erupted from the back of the classroom that I realized my transformation from Calico to Siamese.

I have since learned from that embarrassing incident and am finally taking on the costume constructing myself this year. Galesburg High

School Student Council is hosting Haunted High School on Tuesday, October 28th from 5-7 p.m.

As a member of Student Council, I am required to dress up and pass out candy to the younger ghouls and goblins roaming the halls. Rather than simply tossing a sheet over our heads or throwing on a Superman cape, my good pal Maria and I devised a more creative plan of attack for our outfits. Using a cardboard box and two cans of spray paint found in the back of the garage, invisible tape and a pair of safety scissors, my fellow artist and I created two masterpieces. You can just call us the Rangers, Power Rangers that is. Although a properly fitted Ranger must look good, it is also vital that he or she is ready to bust a move at any moment. In order to prepare for any greedy goblins that will surely come our way, Maria and I have been practicing our signature defensive maneuvers. Twenty-three roundhouse kicks and thirteen karate chops later, we are ready for action! "What's that? No Mom, please put your needle and thread back in the drawer."

My Week as a Power Ranger and Poet

NOVEMBER 1

- -

HAVE YOU EVER HAD ONE OF THOSE WEEKS WHERE IT SEEMS LIKE you're on a unicycle going 90 miles per hour on the Autobahn? You pedal faster and faster with no sense of balance, praying that your momentum will carry you through to Friday without crashing in a pothole on Wednesday. For me, this has been one of those weeks straight off the NASCAR circuit and here on Thursday night I'm still in search of a pit stop.

Filling out my agenda on Sunday night, I also topped off my think tank knowing I would need plenty of mental stamina for the week ahead. With our GHS golf banquet on Tuesday at Lake Bracken, my senior co-captain Abbey and I prepared for our roles during the ceremony. With only 24 hours to become Steven Spielberg, the pressure was on to create a memorable DVD of our golf season. About 85 pictures, three frozen monitors, and four hours later, our cool cinematography made a real dinosaur out of Steve's "Jurassic Park".

I also wore the title of another occupation this week when I transformed into the Green Power Ranger. Unfortunately, Haunted High School fell on the same night as the golf banquet this year, so my chance to round-kick any ghouls was cut short. My quick change from a crime-fighting hero into a formal banquet attendee was an event in itself. Although I was probably still wearing some Green Ranger on my face, I made it to the banquet just in time to fork a big spud at the potato bar and hand out some gag gifts to the underclassmen.

Before I go any further, I must also add that this was the first week of second term. A fresh start was just what I needed to keep my wheels rotating. My three new classes are among the most fun and interesting that I've taken in high school. I start my day doing plie's with leaps and turns like a member of the Nutcracker in Dance I. After busting a move, I cool down by exploring the fascinating minds of filmmakers like Alfred Hitchcock during Film and Video. Third block arrives with the opportunity to analyze, annotate, and compose writing styles from poetry to non-fiction in A.P English. Even though Physics continues to occupy my fourth block slot, a little consistency is nice.

On top of becoming a producer, Power Ranger, and poet, there's still a mountain of college preparation and application looming over my head. But despite the unusual increase in the speed limit these past few days, it's all worth it in the end. This I realized after finishing my final task, reading my acceptance letter from North Central College. I wonder if they allow unicycles on campus?

The Voice of Knowledge

NOVEMBER 8

IN HOMAGE TO THE VOICE ON THE INTERCOM.

You welcome me to school each morning with the Pledge of Allegiance. I know I can always count on you to start my day with a joyful morning "hello." Yes, I may have dropped my strawberry Pop-Tart frosting side down on the gym floor and forgotten to take my P.E. clothes home for the weekend, but you don't mind the smell or my morning demeanor. "Have a magnificent Monday!" you chirp.

Oh, what's this? A black Honda Accord has left its lights on in the parking lot? Why thank you for notifying me, Intercom Voice! Without your thoughtfulness, the Black Pearl may have become a sunken ship searching for jumper cables by the end of 4th block. Intercom Voice, you are a lifesaver!

I miss you during the first half of the day. Where do you go? Surely, you aren't fraternizing with the fire alarm or shooting the breeze with the school bell. No, that cannot be true. Sometimes I hear you calling for other students. Why have you never spoken my name, Intercom Voice? I suppose I'll just wait patiently for that glorious day when your sound waves echo "Jane Simkins" throughout the hallways and classrooms. Until then, well, I guess we'll always have the daily bulletin.

Our advisory time together is very dear to me, my Tickler of the Eardrums. You are always there to give me the 4-1-1 on what's happening at GHS. I know I'll never have to worry about being very far out of the loop. Just today, an underclassman was confused about where the Blood Drive was held and I, having heard your message, sent her skipping with "The Learning Center, my dear." Thanks, I.V.!

Some of my fellow classmates seem to associate you with negative vibes. With the crack of a speaker and the drop of a name, they begin to sweat and bite their nails, praying there is no "report to the principal's office" to follow. But don't you worry about them, my Lord of the Larynx, they are just intimidated by you. If I overhear my friends calling you names, I instantly come to your defense. "How dare you mock the intercom!" I retort. The strange looks and hideous smirks are totally worth it.

After the school day has ended and the final chalkboard has been erased, you hang out in the office, or hallway, or gymnasium, just a button-press away, patiently and dutifully waiting for the morning Pledge. Eventually, you and I will go our separate ways. You will assuredly end up in full volume working some fancy shmancy car lot for BMW or Mercedes-Benz and I will be up until 5 A.M finishing a college term paper. You will always be close to my heart… What's that my dear Intercom Voice? Wait, the principal wants to see me?

A Teacher Who Made It Real

NOVEMBER 15

- -

I HAVE ROAMED THE STREETS OF PARIS, WITNESSED THE CONSTRUC-tion of the Eiffel Tower and toured the chateaus of France. All these extraordinary experiences occurred in a 20-by-20-foot classroom at Galesburg High School. However, my ability to see life across a vast ocean would not have been possible without my professeur de Francais, Monsieur Nusbaum, the real deal.

By "real deal" I mean that Mr. Nusbaum actually lived and stud-ied in France as a student. Rather than popping in an outdated video of ol' Paree, my fellow classmates and I were enchanted daily by his detailed recollections of shopping, eating, sleeping and hanging out in the "Country of Human Rights." The first time I heard Monsieur Nusbaum tell a story about the "no ice in beverages" custom in France, I felt as if I had traveled halfway around the world and cringed at the warm Coca-Cola myself.

With Mr. Nusbaum at the helm, there was rarely a dull moment to be had in French class. When studying entertainment and art, our assign-ment was to create a poster of our favorite film. While learning about French food and dining, designing our own menus reinforced our learn-ing. After translating fairy tales like "Little Red Riding Hood," my class-mates and I put together a puppet show performed in fluent Francais.

A quality sense of humor also made Mr. Nusbaum a "tres fan-tastique" teacher. My first year of French was Mr. Nusbaum's first year with new textbooks. Every now and then, we would come across a corny photo or odd sentence. In most cases, a class would try to ignore pointing out the obviously hilarious sight. Every class, except for French class. Once, we came across a scene of a girl faking a sprained ankle for the word, "tomber" (to fall). Quicker than a cat on a mouse, Monsieur Nusbaum left the class in stitches joking about the image.

Reminiscing on my own memories of Monsieur Nusbaum, I asked my brother what he recollected about his French class. "Mr. Nusbaum brought in this massive fish for Food Day. We all tried some of the fish 'n' chips or, du poisson et frites," he recalled. "He had a unique way of putting the language in its social context, making you feel like you were there. French class was not just memorizing words and phrases."

Along with his obvious passion for teaching and comedic comments, Monsieur Nusbaum never missed an opportunity to share his favorite book, "Le Petite Prince" with his students. I would like to quote a short, but significant excerpt from this lovely story — "What makes the desert beautiful, said the little prince, is that somewhere it hides a well."

Merci and Auvoir, Monsieur Nusbaum.

Editor's note: GHS teacher, Mr. Chad Nusbaum, passed away at home on November 8, 2008 during Jane's senior year.

Lassoed to the Past by Old Letters

NOVEMBER 22

I'VE ALWAYS DREAMED OF TRAVELING BACK IN TIME. THIS THURSDAY, my dream came true. After a long day of dancing, studying Indiana Jones and "Raiders of the Lost Ark," analyzing the poems of Robert Frost, and solving electromagnetic field problems, I was excited for some down time. Straggling in the back door, my mom alerted me that I had a letter. "Oh, just another 'Last offer!' subscription to Cosmo Girl," I assumed. But glancing across the envelope I noticed the handwriting was too informal to be from a magazine company. Upon closer scrutiny, an odd familiarity emerged, as did a curious sense of déjà vu. Looking more intensely at the envelope, I recognized the handwriting as my own. Strangely, my eighth-grade English teacher's name, Mrs. Walker, was printed in the top left-hand corner.

"Could it be?" I wondered amidst my own disbelief. Hands shaking like a washer on spin cycle, I severed the seal. Right then and there, the green-penned letters inside turned to solid gold. Even if they hadn't, what they held was worth all the treasures in the world.

There were two letters. The first one was composed on Sept. 3, 2002 when I was a 4-foot-11-inch, gap-toothed sixth-grader. I liked the idea of blue and white teams, band gave me a headache sometimes, and my friends and I loved riding Courtney's bicycle built for two. Favorite colors were pink and yellow, and boys were… OK.

The second letter was written on May 31, 2005 to the future me. I must admit, I put Miss Cleo to shame with my eighth-grade predictions. "Four years from now I see myself playing two sports, golf and soccer," I had written. I also told myself that I would probably be joining the Marching Streaks my freshman year. "I am going to be playing the mellophone which sounds pretty weird," I noted. Of course, the pre-teen in me also detailed my best friends, secret crush, and favorite baseball team upon the lined paper.

What really tripped my trigger were my outlook and hopes for the rest of my life. "I think high school will be way more fun than junior high because it's bigger and I like the schedule and there are more people. Also, the classes might be more fun. Furthermore, when I get older, I want to be involved with fashion or be a veterinarian. I really hope I do well in high school like my brother, John. I hope when I am a senior, I will be a nice, funny and smart person."

Reliving my junior high thoughts and recognizing my personality in the letter roped me back in time like a lassoed calf. That crush may not have my heart like he did before. Friendships change and grow. That baseball team may not have made it to the World Series. Those goals, though, have stuck with me and become my reality during the past four years.

Apparently, I was about as shallow as an off-season wading pool as I ended the letter with this not so deep closing thought, "I know this is short, but I don't want to have much homework tonight, ha ha!" Some things never change.

Turkey Day Reveries Starring Holiday Films

NOVEMBER 29

THANKSGIVING COMPLETES ME. NOT ONLY IS THE WORD ITSELF A complete combination of noun and verb, but the traditions of the holiday finish off the year in grand style. But no Thanksgiving is complete for me without the Wednesday night church service, Macy's Thanksgiving Day Parade on Thursday morning, the noon gorging, and the afternoon snooze. It was during this latter tryptophan-induced slumber, complete with High Def tuned to the Movie Channel in the background, that my mind drifted into a weird reality-like dream.

Sleepwalking through the channels I noticed certain pieces of films which reminded me of my own family. Coming across "Home Alone," the McAllister family accidentally misses their wake-up call, causing them to almost botch their flight to France. I'm fairly certain my parents would not leave my brother or me halfway across the globe; however, being late does seem to run in the family. Hair dryers whipping around, people dashing out the door with shoes on the wrong feet playing Beat the Train to Church is anything but foreign in the Simkins' house, especially during the holidays. Thank goodness our church has a balcony accessible by the side door for we have yet to see or hear a prelude.

Dream-surfing led me to another of my all-time favorite flicks, "The Incredibles." Obviously, my family is not made up of a bunch of undercover superheroes. Nevertheless, I've got a fairly good idea of what special powers I would anoint on them. My dad's title would be the "Repairer" based upon his amazing ability to fix any broken pipe, door, light switch, you name it. His arch nemesis? That one unlit icicle light that ruins the entire string on the tree. As far as my mom goes, she would be known for her bionic ability to accessorize. Wherever there is a bland outfit to be found, the "Accessorizer" would be there to add that desperate dash of flare. Then we have the Passive-Aggressivator, otherwise known as my brother John. If an argument erupts over whether Rudolph should be an honorary member of the eight reindeer, the Passive-Aggressivator will be there to mumble his opinion under his breath and quickly walk away. Of course, I cannot forget the Barkosaurus, whose real identity happens to be my Australian Shepherd, Boomerang. The special power of the Barkosaurus lies in his ability to scare away every squirrel, bird, and UPS guy that steps foot on the front steps. His arch nemesis? The screen door.

As I unconsciously tune in to "Christmas with the Kranks" and think of my family, well, enough said. Discussions about down-sizing Christmas inevitably develop shortly after Turkey Day at our house, usually about the time Mom asks for the lights to be strung across the roof.

Waking from my short winter's nap, I joyfully discover my most cherished holiday movie of all. Although it may not be in color, this film always manages to bring my family together. I can't exactly put my finger on why I adore it, all I know is this movie always reminds me, "It's a Wonderful Life." Oh, and my special power? That would be my ability to take a "nap" when it's time to wash the dishes after Thanksgiving dinner.

Weekend Update, Simkins-style

DECEMBER 6

- -

IT'S TIME FOR THE WEEKEND UPDATE WITH YOUR HOST, JANE E. Jibber-Jabber. Up first in our news for today where we'll be getting in on the action behind the activities at GHS. Before I begin, I would like to thank the GHS Daily Bulletin for providing me with the information used in this journal entry.

Artte Clubbe kicked off the week by putting their talents on the market with T-shirts, sweatshirts and socks that were truly to "dye for." Every day after school, these artists transformed the cafeteria into a psychedelic shop with their own works of tie-dyed art apparel that could be purchased by faculty and students. Not only will these brilliant clothes give Jack Frost a run for his money, they also provide an opportunity to get a jump on those gift lists!

In other news, Spanish Club members will be spicing it up on the 15th with a "mucho bueno" Christmas party. Room 247 is sure to be the life of the hallways with a fun flick and pizza pizzaz, need I say more? Unfortunately, me no hablo Espanol, so me no eat no pizza. Oh well, I suppose I'll just have to raid the French Club cookies!

What's this? My producer has just informed me that the "Going Green" commission at GHS would like to share some advice on how to help our planet. In order to keep the Earth spinning strong, we must be smart about recycling items such as last week's AP Calculus exam and our empty Gatorade bottles. Keep in mind folks, no one likes a trash talker.

Attention movie goers! On Dec. 9, there will be a discussion session for all you "Twilight" fanatics out there. Make Edward proud and serve up your comments about this and future "Twilight" series films. The chat will be in the library around 7:25 a.m. Be there, share and leave your fangs at home.

Now we'll turn it over to meteorologist, Jane Z. Weathervane for a summary of Wednesday's wacky snowstorm.

Thank you, Jane. Yes, indeedy it seems Mother Nature deemed GHS the blizzard of the month as she stopped by for an extra-large helping during third hour on Wednesday. Students scurried to their cars to remove the deep snow covering their windows. I believe I saw one girl trying to scrape away the snow using a nine-iron. Just as I was about to lend her a broom, a nice young fellow came to the rescue and cleared away the powdery blanket that enveloped her windshield. Let me just say this blizzard was anything but a sweet treat. Back to you, Jane.

That about wraps it up for this morning's newscast, thank you for watching, and the next time you see a tie-dyed rocking, "Twilight" reading, Spanish-speaking student, tell 'em to check out the daily bulletin.

Virginia, Santa is on West Fremont Street

DECEMBER 13

- -

PROJECT HOLIDAY SOUNDS MORE LIKE A SECRET, UNDERCOVER MISsion for James Bond than an assortment of wintry activities organized by Student Council. Here at GHS, we don't just spread the holiday cheer, we shellac it all over our school and community. With our hands decorating the main entry, our voices singing tidings of comfort and joy, and our hearts collecting donations for the angel trees, Stu Co is a holly jolly force to be reckoned with.

Speaking of shellacking, last Friday my fellow Student Council members and I transformed the forlorn front foyer into a "Fa la la" lovely lobby. Scrooge himself would have lit up when he noticed our glorious Christmas tree showered with shiny ornaments from treetop to trunk to stump. Of course, in order to match the realness of "them there balsams," we needed much perseverance. We needed a team to tackle the most physically, mentally and, depending on the length of the string, most emotionally grueling task of all. We needed a light crew. Thankfully, the Thomas Edisons and Bob Villas of the council tackled the tedious task. Those lights were up quicker than you can say, "Ah, what bulb is it this time?" Once the last garland was draped with just the right swag, visitors were mistaking GHS for Center Court at Sandburg Mall.

When we're not dressing up the school during the Christmas season, Stu Co can be found caroling the classics. This Sunday, my fellow members and I will be belting out holiday tunes up and down the hallways of Seminary Manor and Rosewood nursing homes. In apology for our inevitably poor intonation while jingle-bell-rocking, which I blame on the cold and flu season, we hand out candy canes and smiles to our always appreciative audience members.

For those of us who cannot swing a hammer or carry a tune, Stu Co is collecting coed donations during advisories for the angel tree gift boxes. Yes, Virginia, there is a Santa Claus and she or he can be found attending classes on West Fremont Street. Not only do these gifts allow us to share holiday cheer with members of our community, they give all of GHS an opportunity to enjoy the spirit of giving.

Decorating, caroling, and sharing are the ultimate goals of Student Council during the month of December. Phew! I was right, this mission is way too tough for Mr. Bond. After all, the name is Holiday.... Project Holiday. Sure to leave you stirred, not shaken.

Kindness Reigns in Harsh Weather

DECEMBER 20

TWENTY-SEVEN. NOT THE SCORE ON MY ACT, OR THE AMOUNT OF Cheerios I ate for breakfast, but the number of "too close for comfort" meetings I've encountered with the ice and snow this week. From an unplanned cruise past our driveway to fishtailing off the line at the Broad Street stoplight, it appears I'm not the only Streak to have been struck by Mother Nature.

All athletes, whether they're bowlers or basketball players, have felt the wrath of the pre-winter weather. Cancellations of games and practices at the end of the day have become almost routine. My friend Zack told me even sports such as track will have to forego their pre-season indoor workouts. Looks like the only things that will be running this week are noses.

Speaking of noses, the Black Pearl nearly booked a free facial during a few close calls on the slick roads. Flashbacks of driver's ed and my dad's last-minute instructions came in handy Monday when I realized the only way to keep the Black Pearl from spinning around in the intersection was to turn toward the nearest curb. The recent frigid weather has drawn Pearl and me closer. I have formed a love-hate relationship with my defroster, which keeps my windows clear, but my fingers like stalactites. Pearl has also found herself a new home alongside the lawn mower and weed-whacker tucked inside the garage.

My pal Maria mentioned how kind her dad was to don his snow gear and brave the harsh conditions at 6 a.m. to scrape the ice overtaking her windshield like the gloves and mittens blanketing the backseat of my car. Unfortunately, a couple of my comrades didn't make it through the icy battle and unintentionally joined in a game of bumper cars on their way to school. No one's a winner in that game.

Despite the acrimonious weather, I have noticed that at this time of year, the kindness of my classmates seems to shine the brightest. Just yesterday, my buddy Rachel told me her car got stuck in the middle of Fremont Street on her way to school. Thankfully, out of the goodness of his heart, her brother Jake came to the rescue and pushed her car safely back into the drive.

After every big snow, I stay after school for an extra five minutes just to appreciate the nice gestures my fellow classmates show each other. Whether it's a free ride home (thanks, Mrs. S.!), scraping off the neighboring car's windshield or helping someone up after the ice sweeps them off their feet, these random acts of kindness are a great way to outsmart Mother Nature's brutal blows.

One hundred and three. Not the number of snickers I heard after my impromptu execution of a half-lutz on the sidewalk, not the number of pages I have to read over winter break, but the total acts of kindness I witnessed at GHS this week. Take that, Mother Nature!

Togetherness and a Christmas Story

DECEMBER 27

CHRISTMAS MEANS FAMILY FUN, COMPETITION AND HOLIDAY CLASSICS.

"Hey, Mom! What time is "A Christmas Story" on?"

"7 o'clock, John," my mom replies.

"Oh, man, why aren't they playing "A Christmas Story? They've been promoting a 24-hour showing of it," I announce to the empty living room.

"It's not on until 7, Jane," my patient mom echoes from the kitchen.

Five minutes later my oblivious father booms from the basement, "Hey, guys, why aren't we watching "A Christmas Story?"

Christmastime tradition is to my family what the leg lamp (otherwise known as "major award") is to Ralphie's dad on "A Christmas Story." We look forward to showing it off, but it sometimes becomes a "Bumpus" of a burden on my mom.

While quoting every line of this favorite holiday flick blaring in the background, my family and I enjoy piecing together a jigsaw puzzle. For most families, such a puzzle would require zero competitive drive whatsoever, just a relaxing holiday activity. I have had visions of a happy household hovering peacefully over a Scrabble board; Bing Crosby croons "White Christmas" as the fireplace crackles warmly in the corner. The dad nicely offers up his "U" to go with the mom's "Q" and the kids ooh and aah as the dog smiles over the resulting 70-point triple word score. Not my family. At our house, it's every man, woman and child for himself, usually ending with the less cut-throat of us once again suffering the wrath of my dad's smug board game victory. Even a most innocent game of Candy Land becomes a battle for bragging rights.

Every Christmas, I pump myself up, "Jane, this is your year. Every part of that Rudolph puzzle will be placed by YOUR hands alone, up to the 550th piece." Alas, every Christmas Eve at about 11 bells, a shadowy, mustachioed figure lurks behind my chair, scanning my unfinished masterpiece with a keen eye on the final product. Pretending to fix a faulty bulb on the tree, operation Hot Chocolate commences just as Ralphie begins to pummel Scut Farcus. Slowly, Rudolph's nose, a.k.a. piece number 550, slips discretely into the front corduroy pocket. As a result, dear 'ol Dad consistently gets the coup de grace of adding the final piece to my 549 unacknowledged accomplishments.

As a way to work out my jigsaw frustrations, my cousins and I make homemade Christmas gifts for each other. My cousin Amanda always turns my "puzzled" frown upside down with her beyond hilarious wacky crafts. For example, a few laborious Amanda hours had brother John receiving a tastefully assembled vest comprised of nothing but Garry Sheffield baseball cards and love.

Although we may unintentionally spoil movies by practically reading the scripts aloud, over-complicate simple puzzle projects, and don cardboard vests made up of unwanted designated hitters from the Detroit Tigers, we do it together, every year. Now, if you will excuse me, I've got a puzzle piece to stash for next year.

Flying Solo on a Train from Minneapolis

JANUARY 3

AWKWARD SILENCE IS THE SOUNDTRACK OF MY LIFE. WHEN THE phone rings, I always check the caller I.D. just to make sure I feel comfortable communicating with the other party. As a matter of fact, my relationship with the telephone has become so distant and dreaded that I am always relieved to hear the monotone voice of a pre-recorded telemarketing message lessening the pressure of a real conversation. Did I mention I plan to major in communications? Yikes.

Fortunately for me, my two very well-spoken parents have been working with me on my speaking skills whenever the opportunity arises, whether it be a graduation party or a family gathering. "Always ask questions," my mom constantly encourages me. I will admit, this tactic does seem to keep the conversation alive. However, there's a point where interest turns into investigation. Once I've reached about fifteen or so inquiries about the other party's life, add two chairs, a dark room, and a blinding-bright desk lamp and I've just turned my small talk into a CIA examination. "Keep in mind Jane, you want to be interested, not intimidating," I coach myself.

My less than perfect people skills were put to the test Tuesday as I hopped on the 383 Illinois Zephyr on a return trip from Minneapolis after spending a couple days with my brother, John. Oh, and by the way, I was riding solo. No parents to speak on my behalf, navigate our way through Union Station, or offer me a beverage or crossword puzzle. It was Jane and the giant train. It was my personal Independence Day.

The moment I stepped into the rail car, I knew exactly what I was looking for. Two empty seats, one for me, and one for my overstocked stack of magazines which were really serving as a seat filler. Initially, my plan worked like a charm and I happily scanned the pages of Teen Vogue without feeling the need to ask my nonexistent passenger partner how their day went. That was until I met the ticket checker. As he came down the aisle, reviewing everyone's ticket he suddenly paused at mine. "What's this?" he questioned to himself and the other 34 passengers within earshot. Immediately, me being thrown out of a moving train at 80 mph was looking like an impending reality. I searched for my cell phone to dial Parent 911 when the checker laughed and stated, "You seem to have placed your ticket upside down." A sense of humor. Well, I suppose this was a better fate than having train tracks for breakfast. For the rest of the trip, I had a seat partner which wasn't as bad as I had expected. Thank goodness for headphones, the universal sign for "If you speak to me, I probably won't hear you, so enjoy that book."

Upon reaching Union Station, I was forced into dismissing Parenting Rule 101, "never talk to strangers." Much to my surprise, I found my way to Gate F where I proudly held a decent conversation with my bench mate who kindly gave me advice on the importance of keeping a keen eye on my belongings. Although I almost missed my train (see how I just breezed over that bit of information), I was back in Galesburg by 9 p.m. where I witnessed the parents exhaling simultaneously.

My first adventure alone, I felt like a baby bird, kicked out of the nest for the first time. However, with a little help from my parents and some confidence from within, I learned how to fly, even if I hardly made a "peep" the whole way.

Free Writing Cleared the Way

JANUARY 10

- -

YOU KNOW YOU'RE IN TROUBLE WHEN YOU GET WRITER'S BLOCK IN the middle of your own journal. I tried everything. Reading articles from my favorite magazines only gave me the urge to shop. Doodling in the margins turned into an hour-long art project. Crayola was involved. Brainstorming left my imagination in a drought. Even turning to my main musical men, Billy and Elton, failed to leak any lyrical lines onto my barren, college-ruled Mead. The irony of the name "Papermate" inscribed upon my lonely pen struck me with a laugh, followed by an inevitable roll of the eye. What was the deal? Was that perfume I sprayed this morning or creativity repellent?

So, there I sat in utter silence, a starving artist in the making. Suddenly it hit me like a ton of textbooks. The answer to my problem, the bulldozer for the wall barricading my mind from the paper that lay before me surfaced like a jet ski from the abyss of my brain. The impending reality of yet another late night was put to sleep in two words: free writing.

During my sophomore year of English, Mrs. Qualls taught us how to work up a writer's appetite through the exercise of free writing. In the beginning, the idea of simply journalizing anything and everything that came to mind was surprisingly difficult. Breaking the habit of over-thinking sentence structure and sifting through my mental dictionary for the perfect word was its own little nightmare. However, I eventually grew accustomed to the laid-back groove of switching my thoughts to auto pilot while my pencil took control of the navigation. No idea how to bridge a transition from dancing dinosaurs to the morning's breakfast? No worries. Free writing is exactly what it seems, a multitude of memos meant to mellow your mind. Isn't it marvelous?

Free writing served as my staff while I ventured across the daunting lines of my empty notebook and left behind every thought that pursued my congested mind. Thus, it is no surprise as to the success I experienced when free writing cleared my mental path yet again and allowed words to flow from my fingertips and into the computer like a well-oiled machine. I began to wonder if this is the way that the great pianists do it, just start tickling the ivories and ... presto, the unconscious mind begins to waltz its way through Beethoven's Fifth. The trick, it seems to me, is to just jump into the deep end and start swimming, freestyle that is.

I think I'll start expanding this free-writing concept into other areas of my life. What to eat for supper? Just pull out the first thing in the fridge and start going to town. Like riding a bike, don't think about it too much or you'll crash and burn against the boulevard. Stuck in a rut? Just do it! Maybe I'll see if Dad can install an auto-pilot feature on the Black Pearl.

Great Expectations...and then Some

JANUARY 17

- -

IF I COULD PAINT THIS WEEK A COLOR, IT WOULD BE "OUT OF THE blue."

Expecting the unexpected has become my motto these past few days. Thanks to the recent arctic temperatures, school was cancelled Wednesday and Thursday, eliminating final exams for the first time in GHS history (well, at least in my short stint).

No finals? I shut my eyes and hesitantly pinched myself just to make sure I wasn't dreaming. Texts came streaming in from my GHS classmates with the news. After throwing on my specs to verify the latest on the "ticker" er, cell phone, I exhaled in relief like an orca rising to the surface. Looks like the only equations I'll be solving will involve the ratio of hot chocolate to marshmallows. But why do I still feel anxious? Were my grades good enough? Is it too late to turn in my extra credit documentary on George Ohm, the electricity guy?

Although they've been in abundance, snow days aren't the only predictions that have been up in the air lately. By late November, my college applications were mailed to five schools: North Central, St. Louis University, Manhattan College, Lake Forest and Macalester College. I would have thought that the feeling of an over-inflated tire under extreme pressure would have escaped by now. However, the anticipation of the too-big-to-fit-in-our-mailbox acceptance package or the disappointing, standard-enveloped, "We regret to inform you ..." rejection letters have put me over my max P.S.I.

Swirl and prom are also arriving quicker than ever before. Unfortunately, my decisions are not. Swirl will be held on February 14 this year (yes, good ol' Valentine's Day), giving my friends and I about four weeks to line up our dates, our dresses and our dinner reservations. Perhaps we will go for round two of the inter-rotational date group? Or maybe this will be the year I finally get the nerve to ask someone without any outside suggestions, help or technology. Decisions, decisions ...

Loose ends and uncertainty shadow my conscience like a lamp shade disabling me from "seeing the light." However, filing past the distractions and wading through the "what ifs" reminds me of what I know for sure. The Black Pearl will still sparkle from the super wash and wax at Dave's Auto Body, Boomer will continue to insist on a treat upon returning from the great outdoors and Doc Joe will continue to transform shy, gap-toothed girls into confident teeny boppers. As for me, I will come up with a new motto: The sun will come up tomorrow.

Of Self-Defense and Credit Cards
JANUARY 24

- -

BOW TO YOUR SENSEI...OR YOUR SCHEDULE.

Images of Jet Li and Jackie Chan fending off perpetrators using nothing but bare-handed, raw skill as weaponry attacked my snowdrift of a mind. Following an unexpected six-day weekend, my brain was a bowl of mush until the fateful moment when I sat next to my friend Sarah at lunch. As long as I've known Sarah, she's been at the edge of her chair with an appetite to learn. Thus, her comment about beginning Jujitsu classes on Thursday blew past me like the BNSF.

Of course, I couldn't help but be intrigued by her latest expedition. While she went into detail about the technique involved in the art, I tuned in like my favorite FM radio station. This is the point at which the brain train that I had disregarded made a U-turn and struck me with the inspiration engine. Ignoring my extreme physical inflexibility and the seven times I had tripped over myself that day, the words, "Can I join you?" sneaked behind my conscience and escaped from my voice box. Before I could take back my impulse, Sarah had already declared the date, time and place of her, now our, first Jujitsu lesson. Finally, all those years of studying the first "Karate Kid" would be put to uses other than to spiffy up the Black Pearl. Wax on...wax off.

Speaking of learning self-defense, the new school term has armed me with the smarts to protect myself from the worst kind of predator, credit debt. Thanks to my economics teacher, Mr. Schaafsma, I have begun learning the steep downside that inevitably comes with those shiny, keep my cash, credit cards. I am finding that the American Express advice to "not leave home without it" is more economically applied to a few paper presidents in the billfold in the long run. Apparently, bankruptcy hurts more than a roundhouse Jujitsu kick from Sensei.

Along with economics, I have entered the "lively" realm of Lifetime Sports and the more familiar world of Journalism Two. Hence, the variety of transitions rooted among this journal entry. A.P. English remains the lone wolf among the pack of newbies, but it's nice to keep a little continuity in the mix.

As of now, I'm writing as a swift moving, economically aware, lifetime athlete who knows a thing or two about grammar and punctuation. However, I can't help but wonder if Chan and Li are in tune with the annual percentage rate on their Discover cards. Even judo kicks come with a price.

Holy Cow! Whiffle Ball's a Hit!

JANUARY 31

WELL HELLO, EVERYBODY! THIS IS JANARRY CARAY COMING TO YOU live from Wicall Gymnasium where Lifetime Sports and Team Sports have collaborated for the Third Term Wiffle Ball Championship of GHS.

Head coaches Mr. Hart and Mr. Gonzalez are warming the teams up with an intensive 20-minute walk and stretch routine. Is that the butterfly stretch? Holy cow! That's gotta hurt! Speaking of ouch, looks like we've got a couple of uniform malfunctions on the field today. Apparently, Red Shorts' mom forgot to remove his shirt from the hamper again, and it looks like Ima Gonnafall is rounding the bases in ... are those clogs? I suppose they helped her slide into second yesterday, but it's only a matter of time until the shin splints kick in. Speaking of Wednesday's battle of the bats, "Libby's Lions" swept the "Knuth Krushers" and preserved their undefeated title for another day.

Well folks, the ground is wet and the temperatures are frigid. What a bee-yooo-tiful day for Wiffle ball! The two pairs of teams are taking their halves of the field and would you look at that hustle? By golly, I haven't seen running like that since the Cubbies won the series back in 1908. Something tells me the extra pep in their step is related to today's championship award, free Gatorade. Tell me, if the water fountains in the hallway were filled with free Gatorade, would you drink it? I know I would. Shoot, I'd have seconds. Back to the game.

Old Shoeless Joe's stepping up to the plate. His bat appears to be made from the finest blue plastic and the grip, surely constructed by a high-quality duct-tape manufacturer. Here's the wind up, and the pitch ... swing and a miss. Strike one! The rest of the outfield looks to coach Gonzalez for verification of the call. Strike one indeed. Just like the pros, Joe taps the inside of each Nike twice for "good luck" ... or maybe he's trying to get Tracy's Dubble Bubble off his soles. Here's the second wind up, the pitch, and ... it might be, it could be ... it is! A home run by old Shoeless Joe! Holy cow! He even left his trademark, sneakers at home plate. The home team is going wild; high-fives and hoorays all around.

Wait a minute, what's this? I've just been told that the "Bond Barracudas" have brought up their most uncoordinated hitter to lead off the final inning. According to my roster here, her name is Simkins. Standing at five feet, five inches, and with zero coordination her swing is more Tiger Woods than Babe Ruth. Her first hit deflects off the ceiling curtain. Automatic foul ball. Simkins' second swing ends up on the other playing field, literally. Holy Cow! Look out sports fans. They felt the wind from that whiff clear up in Cooperstown! Simkins backwards, let's see, that's Enaj Snikmis. On the two-strike pitch, Simkins wiffles a screamer to deep center, holy cow, it's in the hoop! She really knocked the peanuts and Cracker Jack out of that one! There's the bell ending today's game. Remember folks, even a bad day playin' the old Wiffle beats a good day doin' anything else. Holy Cow!

Concession Crew Comes Through

FEBRUARY 7

- -

WE SERVE YOU YOUR SECOND WIND BETWEEN GAMES. WE CLEAN UP when your attempt at the Allen Iverson shot, sponsored by Gatorade, misses the trash can and plasters the floor with the familiar "movie theater" effect, leaving you to slink away with a look of pure embarrassment.

We sympathize with you on your inability to decide whether your wife is a cheese or pepperoni kind of gal. We remember you with free third quarter hot dogs that we keep stashed in the back of the pizza warmer for our loyal customers. We are your dedicated GHS concession stand workers.

On this night, the Varsity "G" Club will be your hosts for the evening. Mrs. Aten will serve as our fearless and energetic leader. For those who have only experienced the consumer's side of the concession stand table, I would like to take you on a VIP tour behind the scenes of this arsenal of eats.

Whoa there, you mustn't crawl under the table like that. You're in the company of a bona fide concession worker; I will take you through the "Employees Only" entrance. Oh, how I love the smell of melted butter mingling with the distinct aroma of chlorine-saturated swimmer's hair in the evening. Only at our oasis of delights could you bottle up a scent like that. Don't be shy, come follow me to the front lines. It's here in the trenches that the real action takes place. "Two hot dogs, three popcorns, one Snickers, two nachos, and a Pepsi," a good spirited Mrs. Aten relays to the busy bees in back. "Better make that a Diet," informs a hungry but health-conscious customer.

To the left, we have your second half pick-me-ups: a plethora of candy bars, M&M's, and Skittles. Fork over one George Washington for whichever helps you cope with the score of the game. Look away, my dentist friend, Doc Joe. Straight ahead is the almighty nacho station. Its at this very spot that we slather the highest quality tortilla chips with jalapeño cheese from south of the border, and I don't mean Arkansas. This concoction is sure to make your taste buds scream. Forget about unleashing that fiery tongue on the referee until late in the fourth quarter. Then we have the back attack. This area gets its name from the massive amounts of "cooking" and cleaning that takes place here throughout the night. Mr. Henning, how about a varsity letter for concession stand?

Wrapping up our tour, the post-halftime party begins, often chaperoned by Mr. Schwab. The customer door is locked, the floors are swept, and the appliances are sanitized. Oops, looks like we almost forgot to take the trash out. No one likes walking in to 12 empty pizza boxes when they arrive to work in the morning. We may not always be the champions, my friends, but we'll keep on feeding them 'til the end.

Spirit Wall Shows Underclassmen's Resolve

FEBRUARY 14

- -

"IRON CHEF AMERICA" HAS NOTHING ON THE HEATED COMPETITION of our Swirl Week Spirit Wall here at Galesburg High. Before I go any further, let me rewind for a second and school you on the history of the Spirit Wall.

Once upon a time, during the dead of winter, a small group of student council members craved the artistic outlet derived from float building during the week of homecoming. "We must find a way to have a similar creative competition during the week of Swirl," announced a glittery-glued co-ed from the back of the room. Taking this proposal into consideration, the council convened and came up with a project of pure brilliance. According to plans, each class would be assigned a section of wall in the main hallway to show off a unique design reflecting that year's Swirl theme.

These creations would be posted for the student body, faculty and visitors to enjoy as they moseyed through GHS. But of course, there was a catch. Each grade would be allotted only a few hours after school to complete their masterpieces. Did I mention they had only one day? Student council would then recruit non-biased judges to rank the designs from first to fourth places. This is where the students' competitive edge is jolted awake. No self-respecting seniors would dare allow themselves to be shown up by mere underclassmen. Likewise, no self-confident freshman would simply bow down to the big dogs. Thus was born the epic Spirit Wall battle that was alive and kicking this week at GHS.

This year, the rivalry began on what I like to call "Mysterious Monday," mainly because both the juniors and seniors decided to keep our respective entries under wraps from the eyes of underclassmen until the final unveiling. Immediately after school, my friends Maria, Daniel, Jorden and I stationed ourselves at our top-secret decoration location. Occupying the traditional spot in front of the wall for their workshop, the inexperienced competition had nothing to hide. Glitter, paper clippings and random pieces of cellophane snowed from the busy hands of determined participants in our lab. After a hand cramp or three and a couple hours of gluing and snipping, it was alive! Admiring in awe our quick creation, my fellow senior professors, accompanied by two awesome class sponsors, cradled our poster into the main hallway like a blue-ribbon science fair project. The first class done, we couldn't help but take a gander at what we were up against, and boy oh boy, did we ever underestimate our younger competitors!

Putting the "fresh" in freshman, the year nines opted for the splatter paint effect, while the juniors took advantage of the "Masquerade" theme by hanging masks from the top of their poster. A dramatic eye mask dominated the sophomores' wall portion, while our senior project represented a Medieval castle surrounded by "flying masks." Needless to say, keeping our project in hiding was probably unnecessary and may have hurt us in the end, thus proved by the fourth-place ribbon we received the next morning. However, the couple of hours I spent alongside my classmates laughing and comparing paper cuts was worth more than the win, even if we did get "masked" by a few underclassmen.

Music in Time Makes Studying Fine

FEBRUARY 21

- -

WHERE DO YOU STUDY? SOME PEOPLE STUDY IN A BOX, OR ON A rock. Some study in their house, go to their rooms and keep quiet as a mouse. Some study here and there and everywhere! When I study, I listen to music.

Maybe it's the rhythm that helps me keep time, but to prove these thoughts which boggle my mind, I think I'll write this journal in rhyme. My methods may seem a little whack, but this beat is sure to keep me on track. Scanning my economics book, I'm reviewing chapter four; without Run DMC in the background, supply and demand would be a snore. If the price of pizza goes up so does supply; when this question appears on the test, I'll know why. Up next, I must conduct my feature article interview, it's due tomorrow for Journalism II. I asked my friend Sarah, what's your favorite jujitsu move? She took my wrist, flipped me, and then I knew.

It's time for advisory, I'm walking through the halls, up to the second floor to say hi to Mrs. Qualls. She offers me a mint and I show my appreciation through thoughtful words of precise alliteration. Ding! Ding! I hear the 30-second bell ring. Out the door, down the steps, and "Red Rovering" a water fountain line, I barely slide under the radar in time. What's this stuck to my shoe? Is it putty, is it tape, is it Velcro, is it glue? Whatever it is, I'd call it a "Double Bubble" blue.

Sitting at lunch, surrounded by friends, I ask about plans for the coming weekend. Maybe the movies, perhaps a game of Scrabble, either way, we'll end up in a mad gabble. Before I knew it, third block was ahead, and I still had a couple pages of "Hamlet" unread. I should put down the Gatorade and finish Act One, or else next hour may not be so fun.

On my way to Lifetime Sports, I shiver and freeze, the walk to Wicall wouldn't be so bad without this breeze. Entering the gym, I notice the court is split in two, I wonder what activity they have planned for us to do. "This court is hoops, or choose Wiffle Ball," Mr. Hart's voice is echoing off the wall. A few games of wiff, and a round of "Horse" later, block four is over, time to say, "later gator." It's a quick high-five to pal Brian who skies over 6-feet-4, grab my heavy backpack and I'm out the door.

So, as I have fully demonstrated, listening to music keeps me concentrated. The notes flow from my headphones through my brain, and the end result is anything but plain Jane.

Just Grin and Bear It

FEBRUARY 28

- -

HAVE YOU HEARD THE JOKE ABOUT THE 85 ATHLETES CRAMMED INTO an orchestra pit? Well, I can tell you from personal experience that this is no joke, just an ironic location for G-Club to pose for the annual Reflector yearbook picture.

Thursday was Club Picture Day at GHS. Local photographer extraordinaire Bill Dickerson and GHS yearbook adviser Mrs. Aten might call the day something else, let's say "Nightmare on Fremont Street." First, there are about 20 kids firing the same questions nonstop like a flock of sea gulls chasing after one floundering fish. Personally, my short-annoyance span would have taken over and I would have made a call to the megaphone police A.S.A.P. Thankfully, I am not the yearbook adviser. However, I was amazed by Mrs. Aten's ability to simultaneously direct students and answer repetitive questions as if she hadn't already repeated herself. Even my ultra-sensitive sarcasm detector never registered any animosity in her cheery attitude.

I also appreciated her patience with those ants in the pants students who never seem to stand still. I like to call this bunch the "Jumping Sardines." The Jumping Sardine is an interesting character blessed with the inability to hold a pose for more than four seconds. As long as the photographer doesn't hesitate too much between shots, capturing the Jumping Sardine in a state of immobility isn't too difficult. However, sometimes the camera flash quadruples their speed like a hemi in a Volkswagen. Patience is most assuredly a virtue in this situation.

And then there was apathy. Possibly the most frustrating of all are those who refuse to look remotely satisfied with their involvement in the club they're representing. Would it really ruin your image if you appeared happy to be a part of the Champion Scholastic Bowl Team? Was FFA really that traumatic for you? I think not. Hiding your true feelings behind a scowl will be especially tough with the quote, "Science Club rocks my socks!" placed directly above your chemistry comrades. If this label applies to you, do us all a favor next time and just grin and bear it!

When the camera's packed away and the lights go down, it is important that we never forget those who spent their day rounding us up, responding to our redundant inquiries, and waiting patiently for us to look remotely enthused. If they can maintain an 8-hour smile, certainly a 3-second grin should be no problem for us. Unless of course, you're stuck with 85 pairs of pits in the pit.

Here's to You, Mad Morning Dash Girl

MARCH 7

- -

THIS ONE GOES OUT TO THE "BEHIND THE SCENES" FOLKS WHO MAKE every school day morning just a little bit easier.

Dear Mr. Brick-Repair Man, I would sincerely like to show my gratitude for filling in those street ramps that tend to pop up on Prairie from time to time. If it weren't for your excellent and quick paving skills, I would have to strap wings onto the Black Pearl's fender; let me tell you, it's not easy finding a black set of aerodynamic flight gear for Hondas. Meanwhile, your brother, Mr. De-Icer Man, deserves a shout-out for laying down a little love at the intersection at Fremont on those sleety mornings. I'm not the promptest person, but thanks to you, I don't have to worry about serious slide time on those slickened "Purington Pavers" en route to a 7 a.m. student council meeting. My Michelins and I appreciate your efficiency.

Hats off to the friendly drivers who allow me and my 27 classmates to storm the crosswalk from the parking lot to the band doors approximately four minutes prior to the tardy bell each morning. Special kudos to those who refrain from any revving of the engines, "move it or lose it" honks, or piercing stink eyes. When running late, the last thing you want to see is a mean looking pick-up truck challenging you to make a run for it. Fortunately, GHS is home to some of the nicest and mopst empathetic morning drivers who always respect the mad crosswalk dash.

Here's to you, door stopper. Yes you, door stopper. You are so seemingly insignificant being kicked under the corner of the door with your face forever flattened on concrete like that. However, I cannot help but wonder what any of my fellow last-second pack-mules and I would do without your unwavering service. Minus your third hand to clear the way of obstacles, I would no longer hold a zero tardy record. Thanks to you, we can all make it into the classroom a little sooner and safer.

Last, but most certainly not least, I would like to thank my parents. Mom and Dad, also known as alarm clock, daily agenda, motivator and energy provider. I dedicate my mad morning dash to you. With your assistance and somehow always cheerful attitude, I never go to school without a lunch in my backpack and a positive perspective on my mind. If not for you, I would probably still be sleeping.

I have never been one to label myself a "morning person" but with the help of others, even something as small as a rubber doorstop allows me to keep my path clear of obstacles that could skew my direction. In this case, it is painfully apparent to me that it takes a city to raise a child — or at least one frazzled teenage girl ... thanks Galesburg!

A Surprise Dose of Brotherly Love

MARCH 14

- -

A COMBINATION OF DISMAL TEMPERATURES DRIFTING ATOP MOUNtains of homework left me feeling a bit under the weather by Thursday afternoon — and then the doorbell rang. Expecting to find the ever-popular pizza guy, I was astonished to see a familiar face at the window. A face that had been absent from my life since December 27th, to be exact. With a large-for-medium price Happy Joe's pizza in hand and extra-large "gotcha" grin on his face, my brother John stood on the front porch.

At first, I felt as if I were living in a dream. Was my dance partner/instructor, favorite stand-up comedian and personal mentor finally back from the glacial north? I pinched myself just to make sure the surreal moment was, in fact, oh so real. For the first time, my parents succeeded in catching me off guard. Although my mom had been mentioning a possible weekend adventure to visit John, I had our reunion stored for spring break in mid-April. Apparently, a trip from St. Paul, Minnesota, which usually takes about seven hours by Buick (depending on who's behind the wheel), is a mere 45 minutes by plane.

Once I got past the shock and awe, it was like my best friend never left. Only a matter of seconds went by before we broke out the iPods and compared playlists. As usual, the classic dance-off ensued, followed up with a quick cameo by mom's aerobic moves established in the early '80s. Electric Slide or not, I still had some homework to catch up on, which turned into another bonding experience.

For the first time, I was able to hold a legitimate conversation relating to foreign economies with my well-versed brother. Even Third World countries such as Uganda allowed me to contribute something factual to our discussion. It was then that I realized I was growing up. No more days of debating about who should dominate the remote control or whether K'Nex made for a stronger infrastructure than Legos. Same John, new Jane.

Despite spending a few hours together, I was unsure if my brother would still be home when I woke up. It wasn't until I was royally kicked out of his old room that I knew it was real. Ah, the long-lost door in my face sent me stumbling backwards and all was right with the world. Suddenly, the Himalayas of homework disappeared and the sun came out again, because all it takes is a "Good night Janers" from across the hall to remind me that life is good.

And, They're Off!

MARCH 21

- -

AND. HERE. WE. GO.

If high school were the mile race in track, each year would be one
lap around, each term would be the 100-yard dash, and I would be on

the bell lap jogging into the home stretch. Jogging, because although I am excited for the future four years of college, I'm not yet ready to sprint away from GHS. Staring into the eyes of fourth term, I'm reluctantly waving goodbye to my third term classes. In a way, I'm driving with the brakes on.

Waking up in block one with my Journalism II class was always enough to get me going in the morning. Though most people would balk at writing an article that early in the day, my brain got some effective stretching before Economics. Luckily for me and my fellow students, Mrs. Vitale added just the right amount of humor, fun and sometimes even candy for the sleepy-head syndrome. My classmates, though few in number, were the exact kinds of co-eds you would want to be around at 7 a.m. Rarely complaining about assignments or reeking of morning breath, we all worked together and helped each other meet the Budget deadlines.

Speaking of budgets, boy am I going to miss the stocking and bonding of second block Economics! Before the great enlightenment of 2009, also known as the day Mr. Schaafsma taught us about credit cards, I was far from frugal. Not only did we learn to apply the laws of economics to our own pockets, we also explored the financial systems of foreign countries. Hence, my interest in pursuing a Global Studies minor this fall. Initially, I signed up for Econ as nothing more than a filler for my consumer's education requirement. Looking back, what I received from my experience was far more significant and inspiring than I would have ever hoped. In economics lingo, my gain of human capital fully exceeded my expectations.

After advisory and following lunch, it would be easy for me to drift into dreamland. However, with an invigorating class like A.P. English to keep my brain up and running, dozing off was not an option. With the guidance and support of our awesome instructor, Mrs. Wakefield-Bullis, our class was exposed to some of the greatest works of literary merit to hit the shelves. We discovered the man behind the monster in "Frankenstein," followed Oedipus along his journey of fate, and watched Hamlet seek revenge against his stepfather, Claudius. As a class, we struggled and soared through our own journeys, but in the end we all took our capabilities and turned them into possibilities.

Finishing the day off with a few frames of bowling or a relaxing round of wiffleball will be sorely missed in my schedule. Thankfully, my fellow Streaks and I had the opportunity to learn about the benefits of life-time sports from Mr. Hart. Because of the mix of wintry and rainy weather, most of our time was spent inside Wicall Gym. Keeping 70 students occupied in one gym could seem daunting, but the direction and planning skills of Mr. Gonzalez and Mr. Hart assured there was never a wasted moment in sports P.E.

But, there is no looking back as the baton is now firmly in my hand and that of the other seniors at GHS as we round the last turn of the track and gain a glimpse of the finish line. Hitting the straightaway, some of us will be sprinting, many will be jogging, and a painful few will be crawling, but we will all get there together. And as usual, the teachers who got us through the four laps of shin splints and side aches will be running along-side, forever encouraging us through the final stride.

The Smell of the Grass, the Roar of the Crowd

MARCH 28

YOU KNOW WHAT? I LOVE SOCCER. AS A HEATING PAD RESTS ON MY lower back and an ice pack balances on the bridge of my nose, I am still convinced that soccer is the sport for me. Thursday was the start of the girls' soccer season at GHS and this bruise-covered, leg-cramp-suffering senior couldn't be happier.

With new coaches at the helm, the weather on our home turf was perfect. Wait a minute, that can't be right. No crazy walls of wind to run against or finger numbing cold temps? I can actually identify the un-scarfed faces of fans on the sidelines. And I think, oddly, they are smiling.

I am strangely in tune with the 80-minute stop and go sprint in pursuit of the elusive orb, a non-stop, sweat-swimming battle to push the bouncy ball past the opposing 11 players. Where others would become impatient, my teammates and I appreciate the delayed gratification of those three magical seconds where the ball sails past the other goalie's gloves and tucks into the corner of the net. There is absolutely nothing so thrilling as a collision with an opposing player and coming out of the scuffle victorious. So, what if I totally took that shot in the old schnozola instead of my forehead? Being temporarily mistaken for the red-nosed reindeer's twin sister is a small price to pay for an assist.

Besides the action in the game, it is the supportive atmosphere around the perimeter of the field that really grasps my spirit. The shouts of encouragement from our sideline support group push air back in our lungs as we huff and puff like Seabiscuit in the far turn. And just when I'm about to fall over in pure exhaustion, my friends cheer me to keep on trucking. "Go Jane!" my pal Peter shouts from the stands, and immediately I'm back in action with a shot of adrenaline no electrolyte-enriched sports drink can provide. There's no doubt that our families, friends, classmates, coaches and other devotees serve as our 12th man on the field as they put the "fan" in fantastic.

On the north side of our field, opposite the fans section, my teammates and I support each other from our home bench. Coming out for a break from the hustle and bustle, there's always a row of high fives waiting for you as well as a chance to compare notes. "Number 5 is a beast, and 8 has a corner kick that could knock the Statue of Liberty off her block," we chirp back and forth. Sure, we may pass a bit of constructive criticism around the field, but once we hit the bench, our only language is positive encouragement.

I love soccer. Yes, I love telling the other team "good game" at the end of a brutal match and high-fiving the same girl who cleated me moments before. The temporary gloom that comes from a tie game vanishes in the glow of a "job well done" and knuckle pound from our fabulous fan base. Carrying the water cooler back to Wicall with the anticipation of a warm shower waiting for me at home, even the thought of the opposing forces of the heating pad and ice pack bring a smile to my face. Ahhhhhh!

Outdoor Living Reveals True Value of Boys

APRIL 4

BOYS. YOU CAN'T LIVE WITH 'EM, YOU CAN'T HARDLY CANOE ACROSS Lake Storey without 'em. I understood this concept well before my senior year. However, this common piece of knowledge was never apparent to me until I entered the world of Outdoor Living.

Maybe it's because I grew up with my brother for a best friend or simply because boys tend to be more laid back when you backcast your treble hook into their hair. Whatever the reason, I knew my third block was going to be a perfect match when I noticed the lopsided ratio of fishermen to fisherwomen.

Due to the unfavorable weather conditions, our class has spent some quality time out of the water and inside Northgate Lanes. After a few frames with my amigos Brandon, F.J., Peter, Greg and Sam, I found that I tend to step up my game with my bowling brethren behind me. What I would usually think to be an easy-going activity, suddenly became an intense competition. Running low on my average ball-to-pin contact, I sarcastically warned my opponents of my "great skill" with the three-holed sphere. Of course, when I casually obliterated the 10 white towers on the next roll, I acted as though I had expected the strike. Striving to contain my excitement, I did my best to keep a "that was nothing" look on my face. As I returned to the '70s-style rows of seats, Brandon gave me a look of suspicion. Could it be? I shifted toward F.J. and caught another glimpse of skepticism in his eyes. Sometimes I get the feeling that boys have a sixth sense when it comes to sniffing out true athletic ability. But mostly, my arrogance at tenpins is fleeting and my promise to string together a blindfolded 300 on the shoulders of one lucky strike ended up unceremoniously in the gutter on the next throw.

Speaking of striking out, my fellow fellows and I caught nothing but snag fish on our first trip to the banks. As a matter of fact, Lake Storey seemed to be the one hooking us. For instance, when Peter's line became wound around a pesky reed, we held onto Brandon's arm as he branched out to rescue the lure. Another reason boys are often handier than a tackle box to take along to the lake is that they never hesitate to lend a hand, or an arm. Oh, speaking of helping each other out, I should thank F.J. for baiting my hook for me. Unfortunately, I think Mr. Night Crawler turned into a free meal to go as he flew off my line mid-cast. Nevertheless, it is the thought that counts.

Sure, boys can freak you out with the fake fish trick, or pretend to shove you into the murky depths, but I wouldn't trust anyone else on my dock. "Jane, look out it's a piranha!" Ahhh! Wait a minute … a maple leaf? Very funny, boys.

From Rejection to Acceptance

APRIL 11

- -

EVERYTHING HAPPENS FOR A REASON. IN MY EXPERIENCE OF UNFORtunate events, I've found this to be the most common response from any confidant. Is it because they don't want to sound insensitive by telling the truth? That, no, this is not going to be easy to understand much less forget. Or, is it because there really is truth in this oft-used rationalization? That somehow, this seemingly sad twist of fate will guide us in a direction that is a better fit than the previously coveted course. Personally, I'll take the latter.

I was not accepted to my number one college choice. When I read the letter that I had been anticipating/dreading for months, the stark statistic that a lonely one acceptance letter was sent for every 10 applicants stuck me like a thousand freshly sharpened Ticonderogas. Of course, I did have to be honest with myself that my ACT score had me stretching slightly Gumby-like for the opposite outcome. Then again, denial always comes before acceptance. Halfway through a "we hope you will not be discouraged by this," I set the rejection notice down and prepared for my next move ... my dad's shoulder. Very rarely is it that Jane Simkins cries, but on this occasion, my tear levees just weren't strong enough. A girl can be brave for only so long.

After a good third of a Kleenex box mopped up the flood waters, followed by comfort food and "I'm here for you" glances from my furry pal, Boomer, I slumped down at the computer to review my second college choice and reviewed everything from courses of study and clubs, to the football team roster. I was feeling better already. I believe this is also where the whole "acceptance" stage began. Knowing where I was going to study, live and meet new people for my first year of college overpowered the ever-resonating feeling of rejection. Hey, a girl can only sulk for so long.

Further catapulting my excitement for the coming school year were the welcome vibes I felt while attending Admitted Student Day this past Monday at Lake Forest College. Not one for icebreakers, I was a bit nervous when they escorted our parents to another building while 125 of my closest strangers were forced to walk up to one another with questionnaire and Lake Forest red pen in hand, to ask nervous co-eds, "Do you play a sport?" or "Have you traveled farther than 500 miles to be here?" A mere 15 minutes and introductions to a sky diver and tri-lingual kick boxer later, my future classmates suddenly looked much more familiar.

Possibly my favorite part of the day was the opportunity to chat, yes chat, with communications master, Professor Parks. In his book-lined office, my friend, yes friend, Stefano and I, along with two other aspiring Foresters, were able to pick Professor Park's brain about Chicago internships. I was particularly interested when he shared how former students had interned with various Chi-town film companies as well as Rolling Stone magazine. With my dad giving thumbs up to the food in the cafeteria, and the seal of approval trip to the college bookstore, both the Black Pearl and I are now sporting our post-high school academic choice.

So, there it is, living proof that, in fact, things do happen for a reason. However, I'm still looking for the purpose behind the Sun-In fiasco of 2007 — all that came out of that went down the drain, literally.

A List for the Last 23 Days

APRIL 18

- -

MARK MY WORDS. IN THE 23 DAYS THAT REMAIN OF MY HIGH SCHOOL career, I will meet every goal on this "Bucket List." Far more significant than the average grocery list and just as important as my current GPA, this list is a record of the objectives I plan to accomplish by May 20, or before I "kick the bucket" on my senior year.

1. I will review the list of seniors and personally introduce myself to any name or face that appears unfamiliar.

2. I will attend at least one competitive match for each spring sport. However, I must first brush up on my tennis lingo. So far all I've got for cheers are "nice shot" and "look out!"

3. I will pick up every item of trash I see in and around the school. (This applies to all 23 days).

4. I will trade in my PB and J for hot lunch. I must know what all the hype is about this utopian cuisine known as Chicken Nugget Tuesday.

5. I will finally learn how to use the copy machine properly. But first, I will need to discover where the copy machine is hidden.

6. I will purchase that random locker mirror from the school supplies vending machine. The poor thing's sat there staring back at all of us since freshman year.

7. I will time myself on how long it takes to travel from the GAVC wing to the foreign language hall. I will then beat that time, record it and beat it again.

8. I will organize the outdoor living shed. Withholding 35 tangled fishing poles, 22 stinky tackle boxes, and hundreds of other unidentifiable objects from as far back as 1974, this "shed" is the Pandora's Box of GHS.

9. I will claim the closest available parking spot on the strip, even if it means brushing my teeth in Wicall.

10. I will pay my outstanding library fines. Yes, fines with an s.

11. Speaking of returning things, don't worry Mr. Baxter, I'll have that physics book back to you by the end of next week.

12. I will be a proud audience member as I applaud my performing pals in "Annie Get Your Gun" this weekend.

13. I will make my way across the stage at graduation without tripping on or over myself in front of parents, friends, teachers and the viewers at home.

And last, but not least, I will treat every day as if it were my first day of freshman year and I will look at GHS with that same curious perspective. I will un-jam my locker 23 more times, eat 23 more lunches with my friends, and rejoice with 23 more ringings of the dismissal bell. And on the morning of the 24th day, my bucket will have been completely emptied of things to do other than be a Silver Streak for the rest of my days. Hi-Oh Silver, away!

Thanks to Tonight's Production Team

APRIL 25

- -

THERE'S NO "I" IN PROM. SURE, THIS SEASONED HOMECOMING AND Swirl veteran knows her way around her dad's wallet and the best place to anchor a streamer in Thiel gymnasium. But now we are talking about the Johnny Depp of all dances, senior prom. The organization and groundwork involved in crafting "A Black-Tie Affair" commencing tonight began back when we were wee freshmen.

In order to earn a little "prom profits," members of the class of 2009 took their place behind concession stands at both varsity basketball and football games. Filling popcorn bags to the brim, sweeping up that same popcorn, and risking third-degree ego burns from elementary students correcting your change-making skills, all were very small prices to pay in order to reserve Lake Storey Pavilion for our memory-making night. Surprisingly, scrubbing and selling alongside my classmates didn't feel like work at all. Dare I say it was fun?

Speaking of daring, did I mention the bravery of our two class sponsors? It isn't every day you'll find a couple of willing adults to help manage, organize, and paint floats, while also helping to sell candy bars, design spirit walls, and put up with a group of wacky teenagers for four years. Then again, this is not your average teacher and secretary. With the loyalty and never say die enthusiasm from Mrs. Revel and Mrs. Doubet, our senior prom won't take place in a pothole-scarred parking lot with a busted boom box and stale bowl of Chex Mix.

And then there is the prom committee. Have you ever tried bedazzling over 200 invitations? I'm sure my friend Michelle would tell you that after number 30, the "dazzle" is far gone. Not to mention the cutting, tying, folding and envelope stuffing that also went into making the invitations "prom-worthy." By the end of the assembly line, all that remained were a wounded slew of seniors with twice as many paper cuts. Yet, something tells me there were many laughs and "remember whens" exchanged in the process.

Another shout-out goes to the senior parent volunteers who so graciously devoted their time to our "Black Tie Affair." Once again, you pulled through for us just as you've done the past four years. You've been our support group, photographers, extra man in the concession stand, float drivers/builders, and will serve as valets, decorator, and chaperones. Without you, we would be drowning in a pit of papier mache and duct tape with nothing but a motorless hayrack for transportation.

As I round out the list of our senior prom production team, I cannot forget two very dedicated individuals who will devote their night solely to keeping our car keys, cameras, cell phones, stilettos and other miscellaneous items safe. Sarah and Lauren, it was just last year that Jenna and I courageously volunteered for the coat check gig at prom. We shall now pass the plastic hangers on to our brave comrades. My advice would be to keep the brown sacks in order, stay hydrated, and no matter how flustered you may feel by the end of the night, keep smiling, because in a blink of an eye, you will be bedecked and bedazzled at your very own "Black Tie Affair."

School Code Cracked: Just be Yourself

MAY 2

WHAT I'M ABOUT TO TELL YOU IS TOP SECRET INFORMATION THAT cannot be shared with any outsiders. This is to remain between you and me. As my confidant, I am putting my full trust in you that, no matter the circumstances, what is written in the journal, stays in the journal. You have approximately three minutes to read this. Your time starts now.

There are multiple myths about high school and being a teenager in general, so many that we begin to mistake the real for the fake. I call it the "Code of Misconduct." After spending four years as a high school student and six years as a teenager, I've decided to finally crack that code.

Save the drama for your mama. Two years from now, scratch that, two hours from now, you will have forgotten about that girl who accidentally bumped you into the trash can during passing periods. No need to dig the attitude out of the hamper, chances are she did not plan on sending anyone Dumpster diving when she woke up this morning. Oh, and that guy in your gym class who clobbered you with the pickle ball? Yeah, he has a crush on you and would rather cause you brief physical pain than risk a dent to his own shiny ego. It sounds so third grade, right? Exactly, so don't be surprised when your 16-year-old "knight in shining armor" or your "damsel in distress" pulls a switch on you like musical chairs, leaving you alone on the dance floor. Remember, in puppy love, someone eventually grows up to be a dog.

Enough of the mushy gushy sweet talk, are you still with me? Good. Keep reading. ...

There will be popular kids. Will they all be jocks? No. Will they all be jerks? No. Will they all be perfect? Never. Here's the thing about popularity. The ones who call themselves popular, are often not. The ones who are confident in who they are and love what they do are often the most seen and heard. Not because they have a Colgate smile or were born with the ability to kick a ball or sing a song, but simply because they embrace themselves. It's easy to follow in someone's footsteps. Anyone can walk an already beaten path, but their lives will be hidden among the shadow of the original trekker. In less Yoda-like terms, do what you do, how you want to do it, when you want to do it, for why you want to do it. After all, carbon copies tend to be see-through.

The code has officially been cracked. Burn it, lock it up, digest it, mail it, do with it what you will, but whatever you do, don't share it. Because information this valuable can be possessed only by those who seek it.

Thankful for Mom's One-Of-A-Kind Dedication

MAY 9

"MA, MEATLOAF!" THIS WISECRACKING ORDER SHOUTED IN THE movie "Wedding Crashers" is something I would never have the audacity or guts to yell at my own mother. Even though I have a strong admiration for meatloaf, I respect and fear my mom far too much to ever order her around in such a way. Considering what she does for me already, I'm certain I would send myself to my room for that kind of talk.

You see, moms are awesome. But not just for always helping us with constant reminders to take Boomer for a walk, tidy our room or return our physics book to Mr. Baxter (done, I might add); it's really the unspoken ways they teach us to be good people that deserves our gratitude.

My appreciation goes even further than my own mother. There have been numerous teachers who have supported my fellow classmates and me in our studies and future goals that stretch beyond academics. These maternal figures have played a large role in shaping our formative years by pushing us to show up on time, finish what we start and be respectful to ourselves and others. They have been looking over our shoulder and cheering us on after a job well done, even if we colored outside the lines.

Life lessons also have been passed down to me by my two wonderful grandmothers, Mary Sue and Shirley. Grandma Mary Sue taught me how to be patient (forgot to pick me up at Silas once or twice), develop a quick sense of humor and enjoy onions. Grandma Shirley's delivery of chicken and noodles to her buddies when they are sick, the importance of chewing food 27 times (never quite got the hang of that one) and her love of nature, are examples I hope to emulate in my own life. Grandmas love us when we receive a one out of five score on our AP exams. They love us even when we miss the big shot to win the conference title. Heck, they'll even pride themselves on being our "number one fan." They love us on the meanest of Mondays clear through Saturday, get up early on Sunday and start loving us all over again. Now tell me, doesn't that one-of-a-kind dedication deserve a holiday? You're darn right it does.

So, my fellow classmates, teenagers, sons and daughters in general, let's show some love for mom, grandma, godmother, aunt, whoever has mothered you through your journey in life. Just as they do for us, everyday. When you hustle out the door at 7:39 a.m. and your mom wishes you a good day, take the time to wish her one, too. In the long run, it's worth the tardy warning. Oh, and you know how she's always asking how your day was at school? Next time, answer with something a little more informative and interesting than an apathetic, "fine." She asks not because she must, but because she cares.

Mother's Day is certainly a necessary holiday, but it's important to remember to keep the gratitude alive all year round. The next time you want somebody to make you a sandwich, do it yourself. And while you're at it, offer your mom one with a little something extra on it. "Ma, meatloaf?"

She Did It Her Way, Now Do It Yours

MAY 16

- -

AS YOU MAY REALIZE BY NOW, I SOMETIMES EXPRESS MYSELF BEST through the language of music. Browsing the tunes of my music player, I came across a song that I found connected with where I am and how I feel at this moment in my life. With a little bit of tweaking and a night of determination, I personalized the Rat Pack hit "My Way" by Frank Sinatra. So sit back, turn on the rhythm in your mental jukebox, and hit it, Daddio!

> And now, it's finally here
> And so my career at GHS has ended
> My friend, these past four years
> I became more attached than I'd intended
>
> I'll miss my locker, good ol' 615,
> You never once left me in a jam
> What reeks? What's that awful stink?
> Yikes ... it's last week's Swiss and ham

Lessons, I've learned a lot
I've memorized the Periodic Table
I fished, I caught a few knots
But these life skills should keep me stable

I planned each history project
I was Lucy Ball, I was Clara Bow
And when that first hour bell rang
I did not want to go.

Yes rainy days, I had a few
When I wore my squeakiest shoes
I did not pout; the sun would be out
So I smiled and refused all my doubt
I squeaked aloud and I sloshed proud
And dodged the earthworms

I dissected a pig, I airbrushed and drew
I've had my fill of Frost, my share of Hamlets
And now as I conclude
I'll miss those chicken nuggets.

To think I'll hang my hat,
And may I say in full commitment
I'll be back, yes I'll be back
Soon for a visit.

For what is a Streak? For what has she got?
If not her past, then she will be lost
Won't find her way
Through the new
But alone, out in the blue
The yearbook proves
I'm ready to move
Graduation's coming!

There you have it, "My Way" Jane's way. With four days of school ahead of me, it's becoming more and more difficult to put into words, especially on paper, just how I feel. I would encourage other seniors out there to re-lyric a song themselves. After all, you can only get where you want to be by doing it your way.

Thanks for the Memories

MAY 23

"LIKE SANDS THROUGH THE HOURGLASS, SO ARE THE DAYS OF OUR lives."

OK, so maybe that was a little over dramatic. But in some ways, the past week has felt a tad like living in a daytime soap opera. One minute, the people around me are sharing their hopes and dreams, and then before you can say "Congrats, grad!" tears begin to flow like last Friday's downpour. Even I, the girl with the sensitivity of a Canadian lumberjack, turned into a human sprinkler system Wednesday, the final day of class for seniors. Stack on a week of banquets and award presentations filled with powerful speeches, nostalgic slide shows and last-chance bear hugs, and you'll have even The Hulk hogging all the tissues.

As the Week of Jane rolls irreversibly into Sunday, my classmates will inspire us with their past, present and future speeches and the jazz choir will sing its final note, leaving the remains of a cleaned-out Kleenex box at my feet and a Rudolph the Red-nosed Raccoon peering out between my cap and gown. The good thing is, there's about 200 of my fellow classmates rowing in the same emotional boat. I've learned the cure for senioritis is reflecting on the past and, more recently, the remedy for graduation is living in the moment. Thus, my goal these days has been to make as many memories with my friends as I can cram in a photo album, or five.

When it comes to "photo opps" I usually choose to "opp out." However, I've learned to embrace every ceremony and grad party as a Red-Carpet event with my classmates. After the awards assembly Monday, several of my fellow "big cheesers" and I stuck around to capture some rather memorable moments as our proud parents encouraged us to "look over here," "don't blink," or to say, "Graduation." Of course, in these situations, there's always that one person either looking off into the distance or at the back of their eyelids. Not to worry though, Mr. Bennewitz taught me how to Photoshop like a pro back in journalism class. Now that I think of it, this whole week has been one extensive Kodak moment.

Once the cameras went back in their cases at the completion of Baccalaureate on Wednesday, my friend Peter suggested that we all meet at one of our favorite places — and they call her the Dairy Queen. I'm not sure if it was the brain freeze, or just my perception, but everyone finally seemed to be at ease. Napkins were used for spilled milkshakes instead of tears and talks of future plans were all headed in optimistic directions, not doomsday declarations. It was in that moment that I realized how relaxed I was, just enjoying the nice weather with my good pals, being in the present. It was also in that moment that I realized how quickly it had gotten so late. Father Time had tricked me again.

Well, timing is definitely going to place me in a tricky situation Saturday. Our thrilling come-from-behind victory in the soccer regional this past Wednesday places our game today at 4 p.m., which means I will be oh-so-fashionably late (and sweaty) for my own graduation party. No, I mean sweaty and smelly. Hmmm. So, a personal note to those attending ... for your own benefit, you may wish to arrive after 6 p.m.

Making memories on the field, in the classroom, at the DQ — to my fellow GHS graduates, and even those who couldn't make the entire journey with us, I want to say, thanks for the memories. See you in Hegg Auditorium on Sunday afternoon. I'll be the one with the hand full of tissues in one hand while cramming memories in a tower of albums with the other as the last precious grains of high school sand join their pals on the other side.

Mind's Eye Takes a Look Back

MAY 30

- -

THINK ... THINK ... THINK. WHY IS NOTHING COMING TO ME? WHERE IS that cartoon light bulb that's supposed to be shining above my noggin? My mind is a listless Papermate collecting dust inside of an empty desk. My frustration with my own imagination is absorbing even the slightest possibility for an idea. For crying out loud, I've written over 150 of these, one would think that here at the end, writing would be a breeze.

Now that I know how to ride the bike, how do I get off? I really need to stick the dismount. Smack, smack, smack. What's that? Oh, just me trying to wake up my think tank. But still, nothing. My mind is an unpublished novel. No one but me can read what I'm thinking because I, the author, have run out of ink, or in this case, something far less easy to purchase and much more difficult to restock. I'm fresh out of words.

How about a simile or metaphor to start? My high school career up to now has felt like living in a movie. Go with it. Sometimes, life was a comedy in which I often laughed at myself. Falling up the stairs in those heels my mom warned me not to wear, just as a crowd of boys turned the corner, must have been scripted. Then there were those scary scenes when I nearly ran out of the building, yelling in horror at third hour's evil geometry test. Freddy and Jason don't have anything on proofs. And of course, everyone's favorite, the melodrama. I had to take a second look at my surroundings every now and then to make sure I wasn't on the set of Mean Girls.

Thankfully, those sticky situations were cut short after junior year. After comedic moments, the best scenes to shoot were the action-packed thrillers. Winter conditioning allowed me to run through the hallways at top speed as if I were on a secret mission from the principal. Between you and me, sometimes I pretended to be a ninja and performed a quick tuck 'n' roll past the math rooms just for kicks. But on most ordinary Monday through Fridays, the feature presentation on Fremont Street would find me cast in Plain-Jane, documentary film fashion, one among hundreds of actors and directors role-playing between the first and finally final bell of the day.

So, my life was like a movie...and... cut! Why am I still drawing a blank? I feel as though I should leave on a powerful, inspiring note. Every blockbuster ends on a memorable finish. I need Kate Winslett tossing a diamond necklace into the deep blue sea, I need Forrest Gump sitting on a bench while the 40-year-old feather floats away on the breeze, I need Tom Cruise telling me he had me at hello. Something, anything to make this last one last. My reel is almost up, and I'm still left with a silent film.

And that's when I found it. Cue the sports reporter with an idea ... enter Jane Simkins.

"Wow, these past school years have gone by fast! It seems like just yesterday I was heading off to all-day kindergarten at Silas Willard Elementary School, kicking and screaming as my parents struggled to get me out of the van. Now, nine years later, here I am heading off to the Big G — Galesburg High School — and I must admit, I'm nervous."

Hidden behind four years of writing I found the golden ticket. And I don't need Charlie or Mr. Wonka to dance around with it. This one's on me. When you don't know how to end your story, just remember where you started.

Streakin' Past High School
(EPILOGUE)

*J*ane Simkins and Trey Yocum were married in June of 2016 and are currently enjoying Midwestern life in Madison, Wisconsin. These days, Jane's writing about all things outdoors in her job as a marketing specialist for the Wisconsin Department of Natural Resources. Her high school companion, Boomerang, passed away at 14 after shepherding Jane safely through her Streakin' days, college, and graduate school. Trey and Jane keep busy with work and chasing after their two rambunctious dogs, Gryff and Val.